AMERICAN THEOLOGICAL INQUIRY

A Biannual Journal
of
Theology, Culture & History

ISBN: 978-1-4982-0527-6
ISSN: 1941-7624

Gannon Murphy, PhD
General Editor

Glenn Siniscalchi, PhD
Editor, Theology

Samuel J. Youngs, PhD (cand.)
Editor, Book Reviews

ABOUT

American Theological Inquiry (ATI) was formed in 2007 by Gannon Murphy (PhD Theology, Univ. Wales, Trinity Saint David) and Stephen Patrick (PhD Philosophy, Univ. Illinois) to open up space for Christian scholars who affirm the historic Ecumenical Creeds to contribute research throughout the broader Christian scholarly community in North America and the West broadly.

PURPOSE

To provide an inter-tradition forum for scholars who affirm the historic Ecumenical Creeds of Christianity to communicate contemporary theologies, developments, commentaries, and insights pertaining to theology, culture, and history toward elevating Western theological discourse. ATI seeks a *critical* function as much or more so as a quasi-ecumenical one. ATI's intention is not to erase or weaken the distinctives of various ecclesial traditions, but to widen the dialogue and increase inter-tradition understanding while mutually affirming Christ's power to transform culture and the importance of strengthening Western Christianity with particular reference to her historic, creedal roots.

URL: http://www.atijournal.org

Indexing. This periodical is indexed in the ATLA Religion Database®, a product of the American Theological Library Association, 300 S. Wacker Dr., Suite 2100, Chicago, IL 60606, USA. email: atla [at] atla.com, http://www.atla.com.

Distribution. ATI maintains a distribution list of approximately 4,200 readers primarily in the U.S. and U.K., though with some international appeal as well. ATI is also accessed independently through library indexing services more than 6,800 times a year resulting in a total readership of around 11,000. Those on ATI's distribution list receive notification of new issues and a biannual communiqué.

To be added to ATI's distribution list which alerts readers of new issues, send an email to: distribution-list [at] atijournal [dot] org.

Subscriptions. A subscription is not needed to access ATI. Each issue is available free of charge in a PDF format by accessing http://www.atijournal.org/. Print copies are available for purchase from Wipf and Stock Publishers through one of the following means:

Online: http://www.wipfandstock.com
Email: orders [at] wipfandstock [dot] com
Fax: 541-344-1506
Phone: 541-344-1528

Be sure to specify the volume and issue number with your order.

Manuscript submissions should be addressed to the General Editor. Emailed submissions are acceptable (gmurphy [at] atijournal [dot] org). ATI is open to diverse submissions concerning theology, culture, and history from the perspective of historic, creedal Christianity. Particular topics of interest generally include:

- Theology (Biblical, philosophical, historical, and systematic).
- Engagement with Patristical literature.
- Theological, cultural, philosophical, and ecclesial trends in the Western world.
- Perspectives on history from an orthodox viewpoint.
- Philosophical and cultural apologetics.

Book reviews should be submitted to: Samuel Youngs at syoungs [at] atijournal [dot] org or bookreviews [at] atijournal [dot] org

Requirements. Submissions should conform to the following standards:

1. Include your full name, title and/or institutional affiliation, and a brief (one sentence) statement affirming the Ecumenical Creeds of Christendom (Apostles', Athanasian, Nicæno-Constantinopolitan, Chalcedonian). Exceptions are made with reference to the filioque clauses and Athanasian anathemas.

2. The work has not been submitted elsewhere, or, permissory documentation is provided by the previous publisher indicating approval for publication in ATI.

3. Submit MSS or book reviews in a Microsoft Word, RTF, or text format.

Advertising. For information on advertising in *American Theological Inquiry*, visit http://atijournal.org/advertising.htm.

Volume 7, No. 2., August 15, 2014.
Copyright © 2007-2014 *American Theological Inquiry*, All Rights Reserved
Minneapolis, Minnesota

AMERICAN THEOLOGICAL INQUIRY
August 15, 2014
Volume 7, No. 2.

CONTENTS

PATRISTIC READING

Irenaeus on the Origin of Man and Evil *The Demonstration of the Apostolic Preaching*, 11-18	1

ARTICLES

Papal Teaching On John Duns Scotus *Daniel J. Heisey*	3
"We Will All Be Changed": Materiality, Resurrection and Reaping Spiritual Bodies in Origen's *Peri Archon* *Brandon Morgan*	13
The Early Church's Inconsequential View of the Mode of Baptism *Darren M. Slade*	21
What's in a Name? Richard Bauckham, First-Century Palestinian Jewish Names, and the Protoevangelium of James *Michael Strickland*	35

BOOK REVIEWS

The Cambridge History of Christianity, 9 volumes. *Richard Brown*	43
Stephen J. Stein (ed.), *The Cambridge History of Religions in America*, 3 volumes. *Richard Brown*	45
David Cheetham, *Ways of Meeting and the Theology of Religions*. *Samuel Jacob Youngs*	47
Hans Boersma, *Heavenly Participation: The Weaving of a Sacramental Tapestry*. *John Burtka*	50
Sarah Coakley, *God, Sexuality, and the Self: An Essay 'On the Trinity.'* *Derek C. Hatch*	53
Peter T. Sanlon, *Augustine's Theology of Preaching*. *Matthew Hoskin*	55

BOOK REVIEWS (con...)

Christopher M. Hays and Christopher B. Ansberry, eds. *Evangelical Faith and the Challenge of Historical Criticism.*   58

Todd A. Scacewater

ECUMENICAL CREEDS OF THE CHRISTIAN FAITH   63

PATRISTIC READING

Irenaeus on the Origin of Man and Evil
The Demonstration of the Apostolic Preaching, 11-18

[Man was formed with God's own hands], taking from the earth that which was purest and finest, and mingling in measure His own power with the earth. For He traced His own form on the formation, that that which should be seen should be of divine form: for (as) the image of God was man formed and set on the earth. And that he might become living, He breathed on his face the breath of life; that both for the breath and for the formation man should be like unto God. Moreover he was free and self-controlled, being made by God for this end, that he might rule all those things that were upon the earth. And this great created world, prepared by God before the formation of man, was given to man as his place, containing all things within itself. And there were in this place also with (their) tasks the servants of that God who formed all things; and the steward, who was set over all his fellow-servants received this place. Now the servants were angels, and the steward was the archangel.

Now, having made man lord of the earth and all things in it, He secretly appointed him lord also of those who were servants in it. They however were in their perfection; but the lord, that is, man, was (but) small; for he was a child; and it was necessary that he should grow, and so come to (his) perfection. And, that he might have his nourishment and growth with festive and dainty meats, He prepared him a place better than this world, excelling in air, beauty, light, food, plants, fruit, water, and all other necessaries of life: and its name is Paradise. And so fair and good was this Paradise, that the Word of God continually resorted thither, and walked and talked with the man, figuring beforehand the things that should be in the future, (namely) that He should dwell with him and talk with him, and should be with men, teaching them righteousness. But man was a child, not yet having his understanding perfected; wherefore also he was easily led astray by the deceiver.

And, whilst man dwelt in Paradise, God brought before him all living things and commanded him to give names to them all; *and whatsoever Adam called a living soul, that was its name*. And He determined also to make a helper for the man: for thus God said, *It is not good for the man to be alone: let us make for him a helper meet for him.* For among all the other living things there was not found a helper equal and comparable and like to Adam. But God Himself *cast a trance upon Adam and made him sleep;* and, that work might be accomplished from work, since there was no sleep in Paradise, this was brought upon Adam by the will of God; and God *took one of Adam's ribs and filled up the flesh in its place, and the rib which He took He builded into a woman; and so He brought her to Adam;* and he seeing (her) said: *This is now bone of my bone, flesh of my flesh: she shall be called woman, because she was taken from her husband.*

And Adam and Eve—for that is the name of the woman—*were naked, and were not ashamed;* for there was in them an innocent and childlike mind, and it was not possible for them to conceive and understand anything of that which by wickedness through lusts and shameful desires is born in the soul. For they were at that time entire, preserving their own nature; since they had the breath of life which was breathed on their creation: and, while this breath remains in its place and power, it has no comprehension and understanding of things that are base. And therefore they were not ashamed, kissing and embracing each other in purity after the manner of children.

But, lest man should conceive thoughts too high, and be exalted and uplifted, as though he had no lord, because of the authority and freedom granted to him, and so should transgress against his maker God, overpassing his measure, and entertain selfish imaginings of pride in opposition to God; a law was given to him by God, in order that he might perceive that he had as lord the Lord of all. And He set him certain limitations, so that, if he should keep the commandment of God, he should ever remain such as he was, that is to say, immortal; but, if he should not keep it, he should become mortal and be dissolved to earth from whence his formation had been taken. Now the commandment was this: *Of every tree that is in the Paradise thou shalt freely eat; but of that tree alone from which is the knowledge of good and evil, of it thou shalt not eat; for in the day thou eatest, thou shalt surely die.*

This commandment the man kept not, but was disobedient to God, being led astray by the angel who, for the great gifts of God which He had given to man, was envious and jealous of him, and both brought himself to nought and made man sinful, persuading him to disobey the commandment of God. So the angel, becoming by his falsehood the author and originator of sin, himself was struck down, having offended against God, and man he caused to be cast out from Paradise. And, because through the guidance of his disposition he apostatized and departed from God, he was called Satan, according to the Hebrew word; that is, Apostate: but he is also called Slanderer. Now God cursed the serpent which carried and conveyed the Slanderer; and this malediction came on the beast himself and on the angel hidden and concealed in him, even on Satan; and man He put away from His presence, removing him and making him to dwell on the way to Paradise at that time; because Paradise receiveth not the sinful.

And when they were put out of Paradise, Adam and his wife Eve fell into many troubles of anxious grief, going about with sorrow and toil and lamentation in this world. For under the beams of this sun man tilled the earth, and it put forth thorns and thistles, the punishment of sin. Then was fulfilled that which was written: *Adam knew his wife, and she conceived and bare Cain*; and after him *she bare Abel,* Now the apostate angel, who led man into disobedience and made him sinful and caused his expulsion from Paradise, not content with the first evil, wrought a second on the brothers; for filling Cain with his spirit he made him a fratricide. And so Abel died, slain by his brother; signifying thenceforth that certain should be persecuted and oppressed and slain, the unrighteous slaying and persecuting the righteous. And upon this God was angered yet more, and cursed Cain; and it came to pass that everyone of that race in successive generations was made like to the begetter. And God *raised up* another son to Adam, *instead of Abel* who was slain.

And for a very long while wickedness extended and spread, and reached and laid hold upon the whole race of mankind, until a very small seed of righteousness remained among them: and illicit unions took place upon the earth, since angels were united with the daughters of the race of mankind; and they bore to them sons who for their exceeding greatness were called giants. And the angels brought as presents to their wives teachings of wickedness, in that they brought them the virtues of roots and herbs, dyeing in colours and cosmetics, the discovery of rare substances, love-potions, aversions, amours, concupiscence, constraints of love, spells of bewitchment, and all sorcery and idolatry hateful to God; by the entry of which things into the world evil extended and spread, while righteousness was diminished and enfeebled.

PAPAL TEACHING ON JOHN DUNS SCOTUS

Daniel J. Heisey*

Since 1966 three Popes have spoken and written on John Duns Scotus (c. 1266-1308), and this essay traces the history of the development of nearly fifty years of papal teaching. That teaching began right after the close of the Second Vatican Council (1962-1965), but the roots of papal teaching on Scotus go back much farther. Within Catholic intellectual circles, at least, Scotus remains a controversial figure, and part of the historical context for the developing papal teaching on Scotus involves longstanding scholarly misgivings about some of Scotus' ideas and certain interpretations they have received.

Scotus seems to be absent, at least in name, from papal writings before the mid-1960s. For example, although Scotus is associated with defending belief in Mary's Immaculate Conception, he is not mentioned in a century of papal teaching on that dogma. The Apostolic Constitution of Pius IX, *Ineffabilis Deus* (1854), infallibly defining for Catholics that belief, the Encyclical Letter of Pius X, *Ad diem illum laetissimum* (1904), commemorating fifty years of *Ineffabilis Deus*, and the Encyclical Letter of Pius XII, *Fulgens corona* (1953), marking the centenary of *Ineffabilis Deus*, while bearing the stamp of his argument, make no reference to Scotus himself.[1]

This essay considers an Apostolic Letter of Paul VI, *Alma parens* (1966), the homily by John Paul II for the beatification of Scotus (1993), John Paul II's address to members of the Scotus Commission (2002), an Apostolic Letter by Benedict XVI, *Laetare, Colonia Urbs* (2008), and a general audience by Benedict XVI given on Wednesday, 7 July, 2010. These five papal texts place Scotus within the framework established by Vatican I and its Dogmatic Constitution *Dei Filius* (1870), as well as within the scope of Vatican II, especially its decree on ecumenism, *Unitatis redintegratio* (1964).

In 2010 Gonçalo Figueiredo, of the University of Coimbra, surveyed these papal documents on Scotus, giving a summary of each in turn.[2] While noting the role of Scotus in discussions of Christian unity, he concluded that these three post-conciliar Popes were also using Scotus to expand the Church's intellectual reach beyond the realm of Thomism. This present essay, taking into consideration the historical context as well, discerns a corresponding pattern.

---

* Daniel J. Heisey, O. S. B., is a Benedictine monk of Saint Vincent Archabbey, Latrobe, Pennsylvania, where is known as Brother Bruno. A graduate of the University of Cambridge, he teaches Church History at Saint Vincent Seminary.

[1] For Scotus and Mary, see Miri Rubin, *Mother of God: A History of the Virgin Mary* (New Haven and London: Yale University Press, 2009), 303-304; Sarah Jane Boss, "The Development of the Doctrine of Mary's Immaculate Conception," in *Mary: The Complete Resource*, ed. Sarah Jane Boss (Oxford: Oxford University Press, 2007), 212-214; Hilda C. Graef, *Mary: A History of Doctrine and Devotion*, vol. 1 (New York: Sheed and Ward, 1963), 300-302; for Scotus' Mariology, see Luigi Gambero, *Mary in the Middle Ages: The Blessed Virgin Mary in the Thought of Medieval Latin Theologians*, trans. Thomas Buffer (San Francisco: Ignatius Press, 2005), 243-252.

[2] Gonçalo Figueiredo, "Duns Escoto nos Papas pós Concilares," *Itinerarium: Revista Quadrimestral de Cultura* 56 (May/December, 2010): 293-318.

Within the wider context of the two Vatican councils, papal teaching thus far on Scotus indicates his emerging importance for ongoing conversation amongst various Christian communities, particularly on a scholarly level discussing how questions of faith and reason intersect. While proposing and promoting such discussion, the Popes nevertheless have avoided outlining and imposing a detailed agenda for dialogue based on the works of Scotus. Despite enjoying a reputation as a Marian theologian, Scotus' Mariology has played at best a minor role in the ordinary magisterial teaching of Paul VI, John Paul II, and Benedict XVI.

Paul VI and Scotus' Ecumenical Role

The occasion for Paul VI's Apostolic Letter *Alma parens* was a pair of scholarly conferences on Scotus held in mid-September of 1966 at Oxford and Edinburgh.[3] That year was selected to mark 700 years since Scotus' birth. As his name implies, he had hailed from the kingdom of Scotland, his home believed to be the village of Duns in Berwickshire, and after entering the Franciscans, he studied and taught at universities in Oxford, Cambridge (probably), Paris, and Cologne. He died in Cologne and lies entombed in the Franciscan church there. Beyond those points, his biography remains sketchy.[4]

Since those modern conferences were to include scholars and clergy from various Christian communities, Paul VI spoke in general terms about the ecumenical role Scotus could play.[5] In the Pope's view, Scotus' adherence to the Augustinian tradition prevalent within medieval Franciscan thought allowed him to establish common ground with different branches of the Augustinian school which had diverged considerably since the early sixteenth century. When Paul VI wrote *Alma parens*, Vatican II's decree on ecumenism, *Unitatis redintegratio*, was new on the scene and the pope eventually took action when he met officially in Jerusalem with the Orthodox Patriarch Athenagoras and in Rome with the Anglican Archbishop of Canterbury, Michael Ramsey.

---

[3] Paul VI, *Alma parens*, *Acta Apostolicae Sedis* 58 (1966): 609-614; for an English translation (used here), see the Appendix of Stefano M. Manelli, *Blessed John Duns Scotus: Marian Doctor* (New Bedford, MA: Academy of the Immaculate, 2011), 103-110; also "Oxford's Duns Scotus," *The Tablet* (10 September, 1966): 1015; "The Relevance of Scotus," *The Tablet* (17 September, 1966): 1054. See also Hyginus Eugene Cardinale, "The Significance of the Apostolic Letter *Alma parens* of Pope Paul VI," in *De Doctrina Ioannis Duns Scoti: Acta Congressus Scotistici Internationalis Oxonii et Edimburgi, 11-17 Sept. 1966 Celebrati*, ed. , vol. 1, Studia Scholastico-Scotistica 1 (Rome: Commissionis Scotisticae, 1968): 54-61.

[4] Mary Beth Ingham and Mechtild Dreyer, *The Philosophical Vision of John Duns Scotus: An Introduction* (Washington, D. C.: The Catholic University of America Press, 2004), 9-16; Thomas Williams, "Introduction: The Life and Works of John Duns the Scot," in *The Cambridge Companion to Duns Scotus*, ed. Thomas Williams (Cambridge: Cambridge University Press, 2003), 1-6; Richard Cross, *Duns Scotus*, Great Medieval Thinkers (Oxford: Oxford University Press, 1999), 3-4. The sketchiness of Scotus' biography allows for dramatic license, a television film having been produced: *Blessed Duns Scotus: Defender of the Immaculate Conception* (San Francisco: Ignatius Press, 2011); Adriano Braidotti portrayed Scotus. It must be noted that the screen credits explain that a scene wherein Scotus speaks about the Eucharist derives from a meditation by Chiara Lubich (1920-2008). In 2011 this movie won Best Film and Best Actor at the Vatican's second annual Mirabile Dictu International Catholic Film Festival.

[5] The ecumenical theme occurred also in Pacificus Kennedy, "John Duns Scotus: The Subtle Doctor," *The Homiletic and Pastoral Review* 67 (December, 1966): 217; Keith P. O'Brien, "A 'Saint for Europe'," *L'Osservatore Romano*, Weekly Edition in English (12-24 March, 1993): 4.

In *Alma parens,* addressed in large part to British Christians, Paul VI cited a joint declaration made earlier in 1966 in Rome by him and Michael Ramsey. With *Alma parens*, the theology of Scotus thus became another way for Rome to extend what both the King James Version and the Douay-Rheims called "the right hand of fellowship" (Gal 2:9). Cheerful optimism is the general tone of this Apostolic Letter of Paul VI, although Ramsey and his advisors were at a loss what to make of the Pope's suggestion that a thirteenth-century schoolman could serve as the basis for twentieth-century dialogue.[6] Paul VI seems to have been suggesting an interesting topic for further discussion, the details to be worked out in conversation at some unspecified time. In terms of particular points of Scotus' teaching, what exactly he had in mind for such dialogue stands beyond the historian's competence to speculate.

"The teachings of Scotus," wrote Paul VI, "could perhaps provide the golden framework for this serious dialogue between the Catholic Church and the Anglican Communion and the other Christian Communities of Great Britain." Tacitly acknowledging centuries of British Protestant suspicion of Roman Catholicism as the superstitious schema of a hostile foreign monarch, Paul VI pointed out that for three hundred years before the Reformation, Scotus' "doctrine was commonly taught in the schools of Britain, not a foreign imposition but brought to flower on the fertile soil of Scotus' native land. To put emphasis on Scotus' usefulness in furthering modern ecumenical dialogue, the Pope quoted an observation regarding Scotus made by Jean Gerson (1363-1429), that Scotus sought "not to assert himself with quarrelsome singularity, but with humility to establish concord."

However vaguely stated, that concord and fellowship already existed to the extent that all Christians bore common witness to the faith in the fact of critics and doubters in the secular world, and somewhat surprisingly the Pope also noted the place that Scholastic thought could hold in modern discourse. Paul VI pointed to *Aeterni patris* (1879), Leo XIII's encyclical letter on Thomas Aquinas, and said that while Leo XIII encouraged Thomism, he also extolled other Scholastic doctors, with Leo XIII naming as one example Bonaventure. Therefore, Paul VI concluded, Scotus could be ranked among them, though not surpassing or supplanting Aquinas.

It was a daring extrapolation from an encyclical letter advocating that Catholic scholars study and adopt Thomistic thought. Nevertheless, it would appear that Paul VI was seeking to ground his insights about Scotus in the deeper tradition of papal teaching, and he seems to have perceived that Leo XIII intended a broader purpose, the promotion of the Scholastic method in an era marked by empiricism, utilitarianism, and materialism.

Further to the point, Leo XIII, and by extension Paul VI, was ultimately rooting his endorsement of Scholastic thought in a conciliar document from Vatican I, *Dei Filius*, which itself drew upon some fifteen centuries of Catholic intellectual life. Just as Leo XIII had devoted much of his pontificate to interpreting and applying the teachings of Vatican I,[7] so too did Paul VI dedicate a major part of his reign to explaining and implementing those of Vatican II. In so doing, both Popes were aware of centuries of theological continuity, and

---

[6] Owen Chadwick, *Michael Ramsey: A Life* (Oxford: Clarendon Press, 1990), 325. In person, Paul VI reminded Ramsey about the English saints (all medieval) venerated both by Rome and by Canterbury: Peter Hebblethwaite, *Paul VI: The First Modern Pope* (New York: Paulist Press, 1993), 462.

[7] Raymond de Souza, "Two Popes," *First Things* 136 (October, 2003): 36-40.

thus they understood that their respective Church councils depended upon the Council of Trent and its predecessors.

The philosophical perils of the nineteenth century had mutated into more monstrous forms during the twentieth century, and so Paul VI sought to enlist once again Scholasticism against what he called "the black cloud of atheism which hangs darkly over our age." To that end the Pope praised Scotus' "noble attempt to find harmony between natural and supernatural truths." Paul VI's concern over the threat of atheism came six years before his now famous homily of 29 June, 1972, in which he warned that "the smoke of Satan" had entered the Church. From even a year after the Second Vatican Council closed, Paul VI saw that the Church needed to deploy both faith and reason to combat the persistent errors of the post-Enlightenment secular mind, errors that could also infect the sacred.

John Paul II and Scotus' Beatification

Although John Paul II did not cite Duns Scotus in his Marian Encyclical Letter, *Redemptoris Mater* (1987), a few years later he made a significant contribution to the Church's esteem for Scotus, namely for his life of holiness and virtue. In July, 1991, John Paul II declared Scotus to be venerable; in March, 1993, he beatified him. In his homily at Saint Peter's Basilica for the beatification, John Paul II noted that from the time of Scotus' death in 1308 there had been here and there local veneration of him, and said that the glory of the Lord "shines forth in the teaching and holiness of life of Blessed John, minstrel of the Incarnate Word and defender of Mary's Immaculate Conception."[8] This emphasis on personal holiness is to be expected in a homily for someone's beatification, and the Pope explained further why Scotus was important in the late twentieth century.

The Pope observed that although the modern age abounds in "a wealth of human, scientific, and technological resources," many people "have lost a sense of faith and lead a life distant from Christ and his Gospel." In that situation, said the Pope, "Blessed Duns Scotus presents himself not only with his sharp mind and extraordinary ability to penetrate the mystery of God, but also with persuasive power of his holiness of life which for the Church and the whole of humanity makes him a teacher of thought and life." John Paul II quoted from Paul VI's Apostolic Letter *Alma parens* citing the statement by Jean Gerson about Scotus working not to assert himself but to build up concord. John Paul II also quoted Paul VI's words about Scotus helping to combat the dark forces of atheism. With the beatification of John Duns Scotus, we see the ordinary Magisterium of the Church developing, one Pope building upon the teaching of another.

Early in 2002 John Paul II addressed members of the Scotus Commission.[9] While this address was primarily an expression of thanks and an exhortation to these scholars to continue their work of editing and publishing the writings of John Duns Scotus, it reiterated

---

[8] John Paul II, "Christians Follow Different Paths to the Same Destination," *L'Osservatore Romano*, Weekly Edition in English (12-24 March, 1993): 1 and 4; see also John Paul II, "Authentic Witnesses of the Gospel," *The Pope Speaks* 38 (July/August, 1993): 245-248. Quotations here come from the version in the English language edition of *L'Osservatore Romano*.

[9] John Paul II, "Address to the Members of the Scotus Commission," (16 February, 2002); English text, Manelli, *Blessed John Duns Scotus*, 111-113, apparently taken from that found on the Vatican's web site.

the main points made in Paul VI's *Alma parens* and in John Paul II's own homily for Scotus' beatification. Here John Paul II again quoted *Alma parens* on Scotus' role in current ecumenical dialogue, and because of Scotus' balanced use of human reason and divine revelation, the Pope called Scotus "a pillar of Catholic theology." So, by the dawn of the third millennium, three papal documents had set a new course for Catholic assessment of John Duns Scotus.

Excursus: Scotus Before Paul VI and John Paul II

Even though Paul VI cited Leo XIII, this papal attention given to John Duns Scotus seemed to appear without precedent. As we have seen, prior to Paul VI, Scotus went unnamed in papal letters and homilies. Then, in twenty-six years, Scotus went from a rather suspect (or at least problematic) theologian to one being held up by one Pope as an ecumenical example, and then by another Pope as someone worthy of commemoration at the altar. Clearly, these two Popes were charting a sea change in Scotus' reputation within the Catholic Church. To appreciate that change in course, it is worth pausing to review where matters stood before 1966.

By the beginning of the twentieth century Roman Catholic scholars were reserved in their estimation of Scotus, deviating as he did from the conclusions of Thomas Aquinas.[10] Amidst scholarly reticence there had been a sonnet, published posthumously in 1918, by Gerard Manley Hopkins (1844-1889), celebrating Scotus as one "Who fired France for Mary without spot," but Hopkins was then an obscure poet with limited yet loyal admirers.[11] By the time of the pontificate of Paul VI, Étienne Gilson had published a vast and judicious study of Scotus' philosophical work in 1952, comparing and contrasting Scotus and Aquinas.[12] For three decades, both in Rome and in Croatia, Karlo Balić had been editing volumes of Scotus' writings, providing them with prefaces in Latin.[13] Since Paul VI had set in motion papal teaching on Scotus by addressing scholarly conferences in English-speaking lands, our attention here turns to writers in that language.

Let three examples suffice. Writing in the late 1950s, Frederick Copleston, a Jesuit, observed that, "[a]s a positive and constructive system," Scotus' philosophy "belongs to the thirteenth century, the century which witnessed the philosophies of St. Bonaventure and, above all, of St. Thomas;" and yet, "in its critical aspects and in its voluntaristic elements, associated though the latter are with Augustinian-Franciscan tradition, it looks forward to

---

[10] Timothy B. Noone, "Universals and Individuation," in *The Cambridge Companion to Duns Scotus*, 100; Efrem Bettoni, *Duns Scotus: The Basic Principles of His Philosophy*, trans. Bernardine Bonansea (Washington, D. C.: The Catholic University of America Press, 1961), 185-186.

[11] Robert Bridges, ed., *Poems of Gerard Manley Hopkins*, 2nd ed. (London: Oxford University Press, 1931), 40; Elgin W. Mellown, "The Reception of Gerard Manley Hopkins' *Poems*, 1918-30," *Modern Philology* 63 (August, 1965): 38-51; R. V. Young, "Hopkins, Scotus, and the Predication of Being," *Renascence* 42 (Fall, 1989,-Winter, 1990): 35-50.

[12] Étienne Gilson, *Jean Duns Scot: Introduction a ses Positions Fondementales*, Études de Philosophie Médiévale 42 (Paris: Librairie Philosophique J. Vrin, 1952). See also Etienne Gilson, *History of Christian Philosophy in the Middle Ages* (New York: Random House, 1955), 454-464; Etienne Gilson, "Doctrinal History and its Interpretation," *Speculum* 24 (October, 1949): 482-492.

[13] Carolus Balić, ed., *Ioannis Duns Scoti Opera Omnia* (Vatican City: Typis Polyglottis Vaticanis, 1950-). Carolus Balić, ed., *Joannis Duns Scoti: Theologiae Marianae Elementa*, Bibliotheca mariana medii aevi 2 (Šibenik, Yugoslavia: Typographia Kačić, 1933).

the fourteenth century," that of William of Ockham and his Nominalism.[14] He also wrote, "[T]hough Scotus was undoubtedly a man of genius, a thinker of great speculative and analytic ability, one may perhaps say that it was St. Bonaventure who stood nearer in thought, as in time, to the spirit" of Saint Francis of Assisi.[15]

Around the same time, a Benedictine, David Knowles, saw the era and arguments of Scotus as the beginnings of a rift that would lead to the post-Reformation intelligentsia taking as axiomatic that there exists an unbridgeable opposition between faith and reason, science and religion. "Though there is nothing of the sceptic in Duns," Knowles wrote, "and though his theology is in all its basic principles the same as that of Aquinas, the realms of philosophy and theology are beginning to fall apart each into its own focus, in a way unfamiliar to the traditions of both Bonaventure and of Aquinas."[16] Nonetheless, Knowles acknowledged that although the origins of such a conflict can be located during the career of Scotus, he was not its originator. Scotus, Knowles conceded, "was indeed in every way wholly orthodox, whatever may be thought of his influence as a metaphysician or natural theologian."[17]

When writing about the era of the Counter-Reformation, Monsignor Philip Hughes noted the "somewhat startling" deference given to Scotus, as well as to Aquinas and Augustine, by Richard Hooker (c. 1554-1600) in his *Treatise on the Laws of Ecclesiastical Polity*, an eight-volume exposition of the Anglican *via media*.[18] Hughes had explained, in the third volume of his three-volume history of the Church, published in the late 1940s, the troubling metaphysical mistakes that some scholars derived from Scotus' philosophical writings. He then wrote that to know only Scotus' philosophical works "is, of course, to know him barely at all."[19] Hughes encouraged the reader to consider other facets of Scotus' life and work, including his personal holiness. Hughes maintained with conviction that Scotus' holiness would be formally recognized and sanctioned by the Catholic Church.

By implication, Scotus' beatification seemed to set aside the qualms or concerns of orthodox intellectuals, whether chroniclers of the history of philosophy, like Copleston, or the history of religious orders, like Knowles, and meanwhile to vindicate the prescience of a cautious narrative historian like Hughes. Too glib may be what *The Tablet* opined, that

---

[14] Frederick Copleston, *A History of Philosophy*, The Bellarmine Series 12, vol. 2 (London: Burns, Oates, and Washbourne, 1959), 485. See also F. C. Copleston, *A History of Medieval Philosophy* (New York: Harper and Row, 1972), 213-229.

[15] Copleston, *A History of Philosophy*, vol. 2, 242.

[16] David Knowles, *The Evolution of Medieval Thought* (Baltimore: Helicon Press, 1962), 308.

[17] David Knowles, *The Religious Orders in England*, vol. 1 (Cambridge: Cambridge University Press, 1950), 238. See David Knowles, *The Religious Orders in England*, vol. 2 (Cambridge: Cambridge University Press, 1955), 75, making the distinction between Scotus and other Scholastics who sought always to elucidate and clarify the deposit of faith and William of Ockham and others who always sought to criticize and restate it.

[18] Philip Hughes, *The Reformation in England*, vol. 3 (London: Hollis and Carter, 1954), 218.

[19] Philip Hughes, *A History of the Church*, vol. 3 (London: Sheed and Ward, 1947), 119. See Philip Hughes, *A Popular History of the Reformation* (London: Hollis and Carter, 1957), 28-29, where Scotus is presented as "a genius" engaged in an "academic world" that was "seething with a passion for fundamental analysis and criticism."

Scotus' "humanist and Reforming critics, opponents of the medieval schoolmen, who expressed their contempt in the word 'dunce,' have got their comeuppance."[20]

Still, John Paul II giving official recognition of Scotus' holiness and citing Paul VI's commendation of Scotus' Scholasticism could well leave Scotus' Catholic critics disconcerted for some time to come. In the meantime, scholarly interest in Scotus has grown: in 2003 appeared *The Cambridge Companion to Duns Scotus*, and the October, 2005, issue of the journal *Modern Theology*, and the September/December, 2009, issue of the journal *Itinerarium* focused on Scotus.

Benedict XVI and Scotus the Thinker

To mark 700 years since the death of Scotus, Benedict XVI issued in 2008 an Apostolic Letter addressed to Joachim Cardinal Meisner and others participating in a commemorative symposium held in Cologne, where Scotus is buried.[21] In this letter Benedict XVI began by recalling the words of praise for Scotus offered by Paul VI and John Paul II. He then wrote that Scotus distinguished himself "by contributing to the progress of the doctrine of the Church and of human science." Benedict XVI wrote that Scotus combined "piety with scientific research," and so the Pope said that he desired "to remind scholars and everyone, believers and non-believers alike, of the path and method that Scotus followed in order to establish harmony between faith and reason." Here may be an echo of Jean Gerson's comment about humility and concord.

While being "[f]irmly anchored to the Catholic faith," wrote the Pope, "Duns Scotus strove to understand, explain, and defend the truth of the faith in the light of human reason." In so doing, Benedict XVI underscored, Scotus "strove to do nothing other than show the consonance of all truths, natural and supernatural, that come from one and the same Source." Thus mentioning God, the Pope noted that "[t]he primacy of the will sheds light on the fact that God is charity before all else." With an allusion to his first Encyclical Letter, *Deus Caritas Est* (2005), Benedict XVI wrote that he saw "with joy that the unique doctrine of this Blessed keeps a special place for this truth, which we consider principally worthy to be researched and taught in our time." In this brief letter on the relevance of Scotus, Benedict XVI rang out essential themes of faith and reason, truth and love.

Two years later, Benedict XVI also addressed the life and works of Scotus during his weekly general audience, occasions he used for delivering a series of popular lectures on important people and ideas from Church history.[22] On that summer day in 2010, Benedict XVI began by outlining the life of John Duns Scotus and quoted from John Paul II's homily for Scotus' beatification. Benedict XVI then turned to Scotus' teaching, and this address, later published as an essay, stands thus far as the longest papal text on Scotus.

According to Benedict XVI, Scotus' great contributions to theology were his writings on the Incarnation, the Eucharist, and Mary. Scotus argued that, even if there had never been a

---

[20] "A Saint in the Making," *The Tablet* (12 December, 1992): 1568.
[21] Benedict XVI, Apostolic Letter, *Laetare, Colonia Urbs* (28 October, 2008), on the 700th anniversary of the death of Scotus: *Acta Apostolicae Sedis* 101 (2009): 3-6. There is an English translation on the Vatican's web site.
[22] Benedict XVI, *Holy Men and Women of the Middle Ages and Beyond: General Audiences, 13 January, 2010, to 26 January, 2011* (San Francisco: Ignatius Press, 2012), 86-93.

Fall—no original sin—God would still have sent the Son. The Incarnation, said Scotus, was God's ultimate act of love, sending His Son into His creation. For Scotus, because of God's freedom, the Incarnation was not contingent upon human sin.

Because there had been a Fall, however, Christ's redeeming Passion, Death, and Resurrection were provided by God for human salvation. That salvific providence became manifest in the Eucharist. Benedict XVI then noted Scotus' defense, rare among scholars of his day, of Mary's Immaculate Conception. Part of Scotus' importance, said Benedict XVI, is his integrity and also therefore his courage to go against the prevailing scholarly consensus of his day.

As a means of showing that Scholasticism can have a meditative dimension, Benedict XVI told his audience that Scotus' "strongly 'Christocentric' theological vision opens us to contemplation, wonder, and gratitude." Benedict XVI declared that "Christ is the center of history and of the cosmos; it is he who gives meaning, dignity, and value to our lives!" Although Benedict XVI did not quote Paul VI's *Alma parens*, he did quote a homily given by Paul VI in 1970 in Manila. On that occasion Paul VI had spoken of Christ as the center of history and as an inexhaustible source for contemplation.

By way of summary, Benedict XVI touched upon a sensitive point for some reason steered clear of by Paul VI and John Paul II. That is, Benedict XVI noted that Scotus grappled with the question of human intellect and human free will, coming to believe a position at variance with what had been taught by Thomas Aquinas and that had derived from Augustine of Hippo. Scotus saw human freedom as a quality of the will, but he was careful also to see that the will follows the intellect; for him, freedom is not an innate and absolute quality of the will, preceding the intellect.

Later thinkers, however, believing they were building upon Scotus' teaching, invested the will with absolute freedom, apart from the intellect. Scotus' disciples gave the strong impression that Scotism should be associated with the still controversial topics of voluntarism and univocity. Both concepts have been adopted to advance arguments for individualism and relativism, but some modern scholars, such as Richard Cross and Thomas Williams, contend that those conclusions are not necessary results of Scotus' thought. These scholars maintain Scotus' claim for univocal theory, for example, is that it properly applies to logic, not metaphysics.[23]

It would seem that these recent Popes, certainly at least Benedict XVI, consider those points worth discussing. By encouraging scholars to approach Scotus as a model for a way to combine reason and faith, intellect and will, Benedict XVI and his two great predecessors seem also to be guiding but not determining the scholarly conversation. They appear to be

---

[23] See Richard Cross, *Duns Scotus on God*, Ashgate Studies in the History of Philosophical Theology (Aldershot, UK: Ashgate Publishing, 2005), 256-257; Richard Cross, *Duns Scotus*, 37-39. See also Thomas Williams, "The Doctrine of Univocity is True and Salutary," *Modern Theology* 21 (October, 2005): 575-585; Giorgio Pini, "Scotus on Hell," *The Modern Schoolman* 89 (July/October, 2012): 223-241. Related to these subjects is Scotus' understanding of Being: see Cross, *Duns Scotus on God*, 258-259; Cross, *Duns Scotus*, 43-45; Hans Urs von Balthasar, *The Glory of the Lord: A Theological Aesthetics*, vol. 5, trans. Oliver Davies, et al. (San Francisco: Ignatius Press, 1991), 18. Original edition, 1965. See also Hans Urs von Balthasar, *Theo-Logic: Theological Logical Theory*, vol. 3, trans. Graham Harrison (San Francisco: Ignatius Press, 2005), 137-138. Original edition, 1987.

encouraging scholars to revisit, amongst other subjects, those two major disputed questions linked to Scotus and his complicated writings, dense works that earned him the designation of "The Subtle Doctor." To what end that scholarly re-examination could arrive, these recent Popes, learned men in their own right, have left open to wherever honest inquiry may lead.[24]

Conclusion

What emerges from reading these five papal documents is Scotus presented as a scholar and as a basis for ecumenical dialogue. As a representative of how an intellectual can combine faith and reason, Scotus may serve as a reminder of the First Vatican Council's teaching in the Dogmatic Constitution *Dei Filius* about the complementary nature of faith and reason. As a figure of common Augustinian heritage for Catholics and Protestants, Scotus can bear witness to the ecumenical hope expressed in the Second Vatican Council's decree *Unitatis redintegratio*. As a university professor, Scotus' ecumenical appeal seems largely to attract modern academics, but from their learned conferences and publications may grow closer collaboration and deeper understanding amongst Christians outside the academy and of diverse confessions.

A striking innovation was Paul VI's use of Leo XIII's promotion of the Scholastic method employed by Thomas Aquinas to include the Scholasticism of Scotus as well. While Aquinas represented the use of Scholastic disputation to integrate the thought of Aristotle into a Christian system, Scotus used Aristotle and the Scholastic method from within the Platonic and Augustinian traditions. It is worth underlining the fact that for Paul VI the Scholastic method, in particular as handled by Scotus, held apologetic value especially against atheism in the post-conciliar era, although in the decades following that council Catholics seemed to be embarrassed by apologetics, perhaps considering them gauche or at least a faux pas in a new season of ecumenical talks.

Especially from John Paul II attention focused on Scotus' holiness and his Marian devotion, but on the whole, in these five papal documents Scotus' role as a defender of Marian doctrine received less notice. Since for Roman Catholics the question of Mary's Immaculate Conception was infallibly and dogmatically settled in 1854 by Pius IX, these three Popes in the late twentieth and early twenty-first centuries seem to have seen no need to enlist Scotus in defense of that dogma. Rather, those three Popes chose to place emphasis, at times vague, upon other aspects of Scotus' work, and it may be that future Popes will develop that emphasis in weightier ways, such as in an encyclical letter on Scotus or in a homily upon the occasion of his canonization.

---

[24] A point made well by Cross, *Duns Scotus on God*, 10: "I have found working slowly and carefully through Scotus' arguments has provided an unparalleled example of someone thinking painstakingly through a vast range of complex theological issues, and has been an opportunity to learn a great deal from a highly individual, creative, and thoughtful theologian. Scotus' beatification by Pope John Paul II in 1993 is testimony to the esteem in which Scotus' theological method is evidently still held."

"WE WILL ALL BE CHANGED": MATERIALITY, RESURRECTION AND REAPING SPIRITUAL BODIES IN ORIGEN'S *PERI ARCHON*

Brandon Morgan*

A consistent theme throughout Origen's *Peri Archon* (henceforth *PA*), particularly regarding his understanding of creation and consummation, is the nature of the soul's relationship to the body. Discerning the nature of this relationship becomes all the more important when Origen attempts to articulate his account of the resurrection of the body after death. In *PA* III.6.4, Origen inquires more specifically into Paul's notion of a "spiritual body" in I Cor. 15, a passage he references multiple times throughout *PA*, *Contra Celsus* and other writings as evidence for his explanation of the resurrected body and how it relates to physical or earthly bodies, and how human bodies achieve consummation in God (I Cor. 15.28).

While many later critics, Methodius and Epiphanius in particular, accuse Origen of rejecting the Christian affirmation of bodily resurrection, Origen's actual discussion of the belief in bodily resurrection conveys a more nuanced sense of embodiment that hinges on the question of the identity and differentiation between earthly and spiritual bodies. More specifically, Origen is concerned to acknowledge a marked *difference* between physical and resurrected bodies without losing a unique *identity* between them that preserves a continuity of reference. My essay explores Origen's understanding of materiality and resurrection as it applies to his interpretation of Paul's "spiritual body" in *PA* III.6 and other similar passages, thus showing his attempt to account for the problematic of the identity and difference of resurrected bodies. My reading of Origen presses a more sophisticated picture of materiality as vulnerable to God's providential ordering and allows interpretations of Origen as a participant in and not in conflict with, the early development of a Christian attention to human corporeality. While recognizing that Origen's concern is not to construct a fully consistent theological system, I will nevertheless conclude by suggesting how Origen's particular explication of resurrection puts pressure on his often referenced axiom that the consummation of all things in God mirrors the beginning of all things.

Materiality in Flux

Many scholars agree that the most sophisticated statement Origen wrote on resurrection and bodies is in a brief excerpt of a commentary on Psalm 1, quoted in Methodius of Olympus' *On the Resurrection* and preserved in Greek in Epiphanius' *Panarion* 64.[1] In the context of Epiphanius' text, the comments are meant to serve as examples of Origen's heterodox view of resurrected bodies, yet they also preserve a developed response to questions of bodily resurrection, such as whether "all the blood that has been lost in

---

* Brandon Morgan is a PhD student in theology at Baylor University.
[1] For a detailed discussion of this text and its impact on the fourth century Origenist controversy, see Don F. Dechow *Dogma and Mysticism* (Macon, GA: Mercer University Press, 1988), Ch. 12. For overlap regarding further fifth century concerns with "Origenism" and the body, see Elizabeth A. Clark, *The Origenist Controversy: The Cultural Construction of an Early Christian Debate* (Princeton, NJ: Princeton University Press, 1992) and "New Perspectives on the Origenist Controversy: Human Embodiment and Ascetic Strategies" *Church History* 59:2 (June 1990); 145-162.

bleedings will rise with our bodies—and all the flesh that has wasted away in illness."[2] According to Origen, bodies have a "natural mutability" that marks them with a perpetual material fluctuation in accordance with our earthly life. This is also true of the food we eat which changes and becomes part of our bodies. Similarly, when we die and are eaten by other animals, "our bodies too are changed in birds of prey and wild beasts, and become parts of those bodies."[3] Given the continual occurrence of bodily change into the bodies of animals and, in the case of cannibalism, into other human bodies, Origen acknowledges that, by nature, "no body ever has the same material substratum" for a consistent period of time.[4] As food enters, changes, and leaves the body, the material aspects of our bodies are continually in flux according to our material needs.[5] Because of this, Origen likens the body to a river, in which our "material substratum" changes constantly throughout the course of our lives.

Origen's understanding of material bodies as impermanent and undergoing a continual state of change plays a vital role in the earlier arguments of *PA*, in which the existence of bodies "admit of diverse and various changes; to such an extent that it can undergo every kind of transformation" (*PA* II.1.4). Origen's examples here are broadened from human bodies to other kinds of substances. For material change also occurs when wood turns to fire, fire turns to smoke and smoke turns to air. However the difference here is that Origen's explanation of corporeality in *PA* is worked out in distinction from the form of existence in which the Father, Son and Holy Spirit subsist. Indeed, the ability to exist incorporeally belongs to the nature of God alone who does not suffer change (*PA* 1.6.4). So while Origen sometimes appears inconsistent about whether souls can persist without physical bodies, he nevertheless acknowledges that in comparison to God who is pure spirit, all souls obtain a kind of "bodiliness" according to their specific environment. Thus, because bodies undergo change and transformation, God creates and fashions whatever forms and species of the body that accords with someone's particular station on the human journey back to God (*PA* III.6.7).[6] In comparison to God, all souls, including angels, demons, and astral souls, are embodied.

This claim requires nuancing Origen's use of the term "body" and "incorporeal", or recognizing that such terms have an ambiguous nature throughout his writing. Lawrence R. Hennessey, following Henri Crouzel, argues that Origen's use of these terms bears a certain ambiguity because "incorporeality can be understood… in at least two ways: first, it can refer to having no body at all; and second, it can refer to having not an earthly body, but one

---

[2] Frank Williams and Karl Holl eds., *The Panarion of Epiphanius of Salamis: De Fide. Books II and III* (Leiden, Netherlands: Brill Academic Publishing, 2013), 64.12.3.

[3] Ibid., 64.12.6.

[4] Ibid.

[5] See Henry Chadwick, "Origen, Celsus, and the Resurrection of the Body" *Journal of Theological Studies* 14 (1948), 86. "Origen beings from the basic fact that the nature of *soma* is impermanent; it is in a continual state of change and transformation caused by the food which is eaten, absorbed by the body and turned to tissue."

[6] "The bodily nature, however, admits of a change in substance, so that God the Artificer of all things, in whatever work of design or construction or restoration he may wish to engage, has at hand the service of this material for all purposes, and can transform and transfer it into whatever forms and species he desires, as the merit of things demand."

which is subtle and invisible, and so is commonly called incorporeal."[7] If Hennessey and Crouzel are correct, then Origen's account of bodily fluctuation, applying as it does to souls with non-earthly bodies, significantly contributes to his interpretation of the transformation to resurrected "spiritual bodies" in I Cor. 15. Because bodies are by nature vulnerable to change, particularly a change into different resurrected bodies, "the body then as it were renders service to the spirit, into a spiritual condition and quality, especially since the bodily nature…was so made by the Creator that it could easily pass into whatever quality he should wish or the circumstance should demand" (*PA* III.6.6). For Origen, God creates bodies that accord with their specific environment. Indeed, "just as, if we had to become water creatures and lived in the sea, we would surely need gills and the other features of fish, so, as we are to inherit the kingdom of heaven and live in places superior to ours, we must have spiritual bodies."[8] Because the heavenly environment is radically different from the present earthly environment, souls require an alternative sort of body that can accommodate one's surroundings.[9]

Identity and Resurrection

Thus far, I have discussed Origen's view of material bodily fluctuation in order to suggest that his account of resurrection entails a radical transformation from one kind of body into another. Thus, I have accounted for the element of *difference* in Origen's understanding, but what of the identity? If, in Paul's words, we "put on" a different body entirely in the resurrection, what establishes the continuity of identity for Origen? How could my spiritual body be so radically different and yet still mine? Before addressing Origen's interpretation of Pauline resurrection in I Cor. 15, it will be necessary to account for some specific ways Origen preserves the continuity of the soul and its body such that, while it bespeaks radical change, it preserves a form that is continuous with earthly bodies. Origen accomplishes this through the use of specific philosophical notions involving form and principle. According to Henry Chadwick, in seeking to make the idea of resurrection more intelligible to other pagan contemporaries Origen deployed the Stoic conception of the *logos spermatikos*, namely a seminal principle that governs the growth of living organisms and determines the

---

[7] Lawrence R. Hennessey, "Origen of Alexandria: The Fate of the Soul and the Body after Death" *Second Century* 8 (1991), 174. This interpretation is explicit in *PA* I. pref. 8 where Origen claims that the body of Christ is "by nature a fine substance and thin like air, and on this account most people think and speak of it as incorporeal; but the Savior had a body which was solid and capable of being handled. It is customary for everything which is not like this to be termed incorporeal by the more simple and uneducated of men, just as the air we breathe may be called incorporeal because it is not a body that can be grasped or held or that can resist pressure." Also see Henry Chadwick, "Origen, Celsus, and the Resurrection of the Body", 86. "Origen begins from the basic fact that the nature of *soma* is impermanent; it is in a continual state of change and transformation…" and M. J. Edwards "Origen No Gnostic, or, on the Incorporeality of Man" *Journal of Theological Studies* 43:1 (1992); 23-57.

[8] Epiphanius, *Panarion* 64.14.7.

[9] See also *Contra Celsum*, Ante-Nicene Fathers 10 vol. (Peabody MA: Hendrickson Publishers), 7.32. "[W]e know that the soul, which is immaterial and invisible by nature, exists in no material place, without having a body suited to the nature of that place. Accordingly, it at one time puts off one body which was necessary before, but which is no longer adequate in its changed state, and it exchanges if for a second; and at another time it assumes another in addition to the former, which is needed as a better covering, suited to the purer ethereal regions of heaven."

development of bodies.[10] This notion is used both in *PA* and *Contra Celsum* as a way of accounting for the continuous nature of bodies between earthly and spiritual states. In Joseph Trigg's words, "It is the seminal principle which will persist from the physical to the spiritual body, producing, of course, a very different body in new conditions of existence."[11]

It becomes possible through the adoption of the philosophical notion of a seminal or life principle to interpret the change between earthly and spiritual bodies without necessarily sacrificing a kind of continuity. Returning again to Origen's comments on Romans 1, "the real Peter and Paul, so to speak, is always the same…even if the nature of the body is in a state of flux, because the form (*eidos*) characterizing the body is the same…"[12] Thus the *eidos* of the person is sustainable throughout ordinary bodily changes by developing according to the *logos spermatikos* implanted within the body. Referencing Paul on the issue of resurrection (I Cor. 15:42-44) just as a seed is planted into the ground, dies, and rises as a stalk of wheat, so the body dies and rises as a spiritual body without forfeiting its common identity with its previous earthly form.

However, in Origen's case, the use of the notion of form and principle bears specific theological connotations since the "life-principle" is associated with God's providential agency over the fluctuating nature of the body. Hence,

> …although the bodies die and are corrupted and scattered, nevertheless by the word of God that same life principle which has all along been preserved in the essence of the body raises them up from the earth and restores and refashions them, just as the power which exists in a grain of wheat refashions and restores the grain, after its corruption and death, into a body with stalk and ear…the life-principle before mentioned, by which the body is refashioned, at the command of God refashions out of the earthly and natural body a spiritual body, which can dwell in the heavens (*PA* II.10.3).

Here Origen adopts the notion of an implanted *logos* governed by God as Creator, which allows him to index his incorporation of the *logos spermatikos* to God's commanding will over the changing nature of the body and, thus, to resurrected bodies. In a similar remark in *Contra Celsus*, Origen again associates the changing nature of bodies with the creative will of God via the life-principle to conclude that Jesus' body was transformed "into one that was ethereal and divine" according to God's providential agency over Christ's body.[13]

Therefore, when Caroline Walker Bynum suggests that Origen's adoption of the Stoic seminal principle implies "a pattern that organizes the flux of matter and yet has its own

---

[10] See Chadwick, "Origen, Celsus, and Resurrection", 101. Also see the discussion of this notion in Joseph Trigg, *Origen: The Bible and Philosophy in the Third-Century Church* (Atlanta, GA: John Knox Press, 1983), 114; Caroline Walker Bynum, *The Resurrection of the Body in Western Christianity, 200-1336* (New York, NY: Columbia University Press, 1995), 66; and the article on "Resurrection" by Brian E. Daley, S.J. in John Anthony McGuckin ed., *The Westminster Handbook to Origen* (Louisville, KY: Westminster John Knox Press, 2004), 184.

[11] Trigg, *Origen*, 114. For the use of this notion in Origen see *PA* II.10.3 and *Contra Celsum* 3.31, 4.57 and 6.77.

[12] Epiphanius, *Panarion*, 64.14.

[13] *Contra Celsus* 3.41.

inherent capacity for growth"[14], she apparently sidesteps the relationship between this principle and God's agency over the providential changes of the body according to desert. The principle finds its nascence within the creative capacity of God over the material flux of bodies, whose will it is to educate souls back to Godself via the pedagogical means of embodiment and the act of resurrection. In this interpretation of Origen, to say that growth and process "belong to the self [and are] fully real and could be fully good"[15] not only speaks of the internal capacity of the body to preserve its identity through fluctuation, but that God's own *logos* furnished the proper goodness of the *eidos* of bodies both within the created world and within the consummation of the soul back to God. In this way, the life-principle bears relation to Origen's description of creation and consummation in which the image of God implanted within humanity induces development, not for the sake of the goodness of process and change *per se*, but toward the reconstitution of the spiritual body when the image of God conforms us to the likeness of God (*PA* III.6.1).

Paul on the Spiritual Body

In light of the forgoing discussion of materiality and the form and principle of the body, Origen's version of bodily resurrection comes more clearly into focus. In *PA* II.3, Origen describes three different possible options for explicating consummation and bodily resurrection. The first consists in the belief in a physical world beyond the one in which humans currently live and in which humans will be resurrected with earthly bodies like those of the present world. The second consists in the belief that earthly bodies will be changed "in proportion to the quality or merits of those who wear it, into an ethereal condition, according to the apostle's saying, 'and we shall be changed' (I Cor. 15.52), and will shine with light" (*PA* II.3.7). The third option entails that souls exist without bodies at all, in which case "the use of bodies will cease; and if this happens, bodily nature returns to non-existence, just as formerly it did not exist" (*PA* II.3.3).

While Origen leaves it up to the reader to choose the option that is most convincing, his reading of I Cor. 15 suggests that Origen holds to the perpetuity of bodiliness after resurrection, though of a particularly ethereal sort. This is more evident when Paul's passage is read through the framework of material flux and the seminal principle explicated in the previous sections. This framework allows Origen to develop a reading of Paul's reference to the *soma pneumatikon* as both different from and yet in continuity with earthly bodies and thus entailing a rejection of the belief in the destruction of substance. Hence, bodies

> ...suffer change and difference of such a kind as to be placed in better or worse positions in accordance with their merits; but things which were made by God for the purpose of permanent existence cannot suffer a destruction of their substance. Those things which in the opinion of the common people are believed to perish have not really perished, as the principles of our faith and of the truth alike agree (*PA* III.6.5).

Death, for Origen, only causes a change in the substance of material bodies and not their outright destruction. It is perhaps fortuitous that Paul uses the example of a seed that dies and returns as a stalk of wheat, for it allows Origen to interpret Paul's example as an analogy for the *logos spermatikos* of the body. In this interpretation, the principle or "seed" is sown as a

---
[14] Bynum, *The Resurrection of the Body in Western Christianity*, 66.
[15] Ibid.

"physical body and raised a spiritual body. If there is a physical body, there is also a spiritual body" (I Cor. 15.44). The life-principle established through God's creation of the physical body and God's transformation of that body in resurrection preserves the form (*eidos*) of the body in the wake of its corporeal transformation. Taking Paul seriously, Origen assumes that the spiritual body first requires the soul's embodiment within an earthly body, "for it is not the spiritual that is first, but the physical and then the spiritual" (I Cor. 15.46). Thus, what is sown is perishable, but what is raised is imperishable. What is sown in weakness is raised in power. Because bodily form is preserved through the perpetuity of the principle of development,

> ...there is not one body which we now use in lowliness and corruption and weakness, and a different one which we are to use hereafter in incorruption and power and glory, but that this same body, having cast off the weaknesses of its present existence, will be transformed into a thing of glory and made spiritual... (*PA* III.6.6).

In light of this interpretation, Origen acknowledges that resurrected bodies will be significantly different from earthly bodies in that they will require a specific transformation for the accommodation of a new environment. Nevertheless, Origen appears to acknowledge the perpetuity of bodily existence (of sorts) after the resurrection and thus, maintains through the theological use of the continuity of form (*eidos*) and the seminal principle of development (*logos spermatikos*) a unity of identity amid the radical transformation of material bodies into spiritual bodies. While later critics of Origen will be unsatisfied with his version of bodily resurrection, suggesting that his interpretation of the spiritual body is insufficiently physical, his attempt to explicate a nuanced and biblical account of resurrection that appears to side against an axiomatic rejection of bodily existence warrants reading Origen as a participant in the gradual development of the Christian attention to embodiment and not a detractor.

Conclusion

I conclude by asking whether Origen's affirmation of bodily resurrection through his reading of Paul's *soma pneumatikon* remains consistent with his view of *apokatastasis*. Multiple times in *Peri Archon*, Origen upholds the principle that the end is like the beginning, which suggests that the consummation of all things will mirror the state at the beginning of all things. Origen uses elements gleaned from his description of creation in order to further explicate issues in his version of consummation and vise-versa, an interpretive strategy that suggests his further commitment to this axiomatic claim. However, if Origen holds that the spiritual bodies of resurrection obtain in the consummation of souls returning to God, this puts pressure on his ability to hold this axiom with consistency.

Joseph Trigg raises a similar question in a remark about Origen's three versions of resurrection. He states, "[I]f the end really is like the beginning, the third possibility—that material, bodily existence will cease when God is all in all—must be his preference."[16] Contra Trigg, I have argued that Origen would actually prefer the second version, which suggests that souls will not exist without some sort of body that retains the form of earthly bodies. While this may not be a significantly different conclusion from the total rejection of bodily existence in light of our contemporary concerns with embodiment and its material

---

[16] Trigg, *Origen*, 112.

nature, Origen wants to make a distinction that, in his own context, presses an early Christian attention to bodily life. Should Origen continue to hold to the axiom that the end is like the beginning, his belief that "intelligences" existed without specific bodily form prior to the creation of the physical world would require him to reject any form of bodiliness, spiritual or otherwise, in the consummation of all things. Since I have tried to show that he appears to hold a form of bodiliness, this raises the question of what is at stake for such a conclusion. Perhaps one would be Origen's willingness to sideline a systematic commitment to the axiom in light of biblical revelation. Thus, in his attempt to account for I Cor.15, he willingly marginalizes the axiom in order to preserve Paul's sense of resurrected bodies. No doubt another would rest in Origen's ability to make a Christian response to other philosophical traditions that view embodiment as necessarily evil. While Origen does suggest that embodiment is a product of the fall, his position nevertheless allows embodiment to contribute to the purification of the soul as it returns to God, so much so that its form in its earthly state is preserved in continuity with its spiritual state. Surely that conclusion would be a development in the right direction.

THE EARLY CHURCH'S INCONSEQUENTIAL VIEW OF THE MODE OF BAPTISM

Darren M. Slade*

David Wright explains that the ancient church placed stringent expectations on the baptismal ceremony, remarking, "Primitive Christianity apparently made baptism accessible only to the most serious and committed candidates. It seems as if the early church was more concerned to weed out and deter than to attract and welcome."[1] These scrupulous beliefs about baptism are evident in some of the church's earliest literature, which associated its salvific effects only with a mature faith in Christ. The early writings emphasized the blood of Jesus (*Barn.* 5), repentance (*Herm. Vis.* 3.7), a confession of faith (*Did.* 7.1, 3), and several years of biblical and spiritual instruction prior to the ceremony (*Trad. ap.* 17). These writers believed the baptismal waters had no salvific properties apart from God (*Dial.* 14), and the ceremony was considered a seal and completion of the sanctification process (*Protr.* 11-12; *Paed.* 1.6). Similarly, the early church stressed the appropriate administration of the baptismal rite while contending against the ceremonies of other schismatic groups.[2]

Recognizing this strong devotion to the proper execution of church ordinances, it would be understandable to conclude that the ancient church was also concerned about the precise mode of baptism as well. The purpose of this article is to examine the extrabiblical evidence from the ancient church to answer which mode of baptism was most common and whether that mode was of any consequence to the early church. However, there is a necessary limit to the scope of this investigation. As H. J. Carpenter remarks, "Few aspects of the life of the Church escaped significant change in the fourth century. In the new conditions of that period, ecclesiastical organization, the formulation of doctrine, the manner of dealing with heresy, and the development of liturgical forms all entered on a new phase."[3] Thus, this research will consult only the writings that existed prior to the fourth century.

The initial section of this article will define four ecclesiological terms relating to baptism: partial immersion, affusion, aspersion, and submersion (total immersion). The second section will address the writings of the subapostolic era (AD 70-150), while the third segment will treat writings from the ante-Nicene period (AD 150-300). The final section will then present a practical application of the research for contemporary churches. In the end, the evidence demonstrates that the early church favored immersion practices prior to the fourth century. However, the investigation cannot definitively prove whether that mode of baptism was partial or total immersion. Ultimately, the early church considered the method

---

* Darren M. Slade, MATS, MDiv, is also the author of "*Arabia Haeresium Ferax* (Arabia Bearer of Heresies): Schismatic Christianity's Potential Influence on Muhammad and the Qur'an", *American Theological Inquiry* (Vol 7, No. 1, January 15, 2014), pp. 43-53.

[1] David F. Wright, "The Baptismal Community," *Bibliotheca Sacra* 160, no. 637 (January 2003): 5.
[2] See Everett Ferguson, *Baptism in the Early Church: History, Theology, and Liturgy in the First Five Centuries* (Grand Rapids, MI: William B. Eerdmans Publishing Company, 2009), 380-99.
[3] H. J. Carpenter, "Creeds and Baptismal Rites in the First Four Centuries," in *Studies in Early Christianity: A Collection of Scholarly Essays*, ed. Everett Ferguson, David M. Scholer, and Paul Corby Finney, vol. 11, *Conversion, Catechumenate, and Baptism in the Early Church* (New York: Garland Publishing, 1993), 367.

of water baptism inconsequential and focused, instead, on the genuineness of the candidate's faith in Christ.

Baptismal Definitions

There are four primary modes of baptism in early Christian tradition: partial immersion, affusion, aspersion, and submersion.[4] Partial immersion is the practice of submerging only part of the body in water while having additional liquid poured over the head. This method should not be confused with the discipline of submersion. Affusion is the exercise of pouring water solely over the baptismal candidate's head; it is sometimes referred to as infusion. In contrast to partial immersion, the rest of the candidate's body is not submerged in water. The act of aspersion involves sprinkling the person with liquid using either the hands or a customary object such as leaf stalks. Candidates are not placed in water nor do they have water poured on them. Submersion, on the other hand, is the practice of covering the candidate's entire body with the baptismal waters. Many commentators refer to this method as "full body" or "total immersion."[5]

Subapostolic Writings (AD 70-150)

The writings of the subapostolic era demonstrate that the early fathers favored immersing the catechumen outdoors in running water.[6] Be that as it may, the writings do not conclusively resolve whether they practiced partial immersion or total submersion most often. The writings of the early church conclude that they regularly accepted affusion as a form of baptism, but it was not the ideal method. The writings also validate that the early church was generally apathetic and indifferent about which particular mode of baptism they practiced.

The Epistle of Barnabas (ca. AD 70-138)[7]

The *Epistle of Barnabas* makes two specific references to the implementation of baptism.

---

[4] This report will follow F. L. Cross and Elizabeth Livingstone's distinction between the four modes of baptism, though this article replaces the term "immersion" with the more specific designation "partial immersion." See F. L. Cross and E. A. Livingstone, eds., *The Oxford Dictionary of the Christian Church*, 3rd ed. (New York: Oxford University Press, 2005), 24, 116, 827, 1563.

[5] The generic term "immersion" is often used to refer to submersion in many resources. In this report, however, the broad designation "immersion" will refer to both "partial" and "total" immersion practices.

[6] Robert Grant defines the "catechumen" as candidates preparing for the rite of baptism through spiritual instruction and discipline. A "petitioner" or "competente" is a candidate in the final weeks before the actual baptismal ceremony and is synonymous with catechumen. See Robert M. Grant, "Development of the Christian Catechumenate," in *Made, Not Born* (Notre Dame, IN: University of Notre Dame Press, 1976), 41-44, 227-28, 251.

[7] John Robinson dates *Barnabas* to the reign of Emperor Vespasian between AD 70-79, which would make it one of the earliest Christian writings outside the New Testament (John A. T. Robinson, *Redating the New Testament* [Philadelphia: Westminster Press, 1976], 313-19). Similarly, Peter Richardson and Martin Shukster ascribe the document to the reign of Emperor Nerva between AD 96-98 (Peter Richardson and Martin B. Shukster, "Barnabas, Nerva and The Yavnean Rabbis," *Journal of Theological Studies* 34, no. 1 [April 1983]: 38-41). However, contemporary scholarship favors a date during the reign of Emperor Hadrian between AD 117-138 (see James Carleton Paget, "The Epistle of Barnabas," *Expository Times* 117, no. 11 [August 2006]: 442-43.)

The author described the process, "Blessed are those who, having set their hope on the cross, descended into the water [κατέβησαν εἰς τὸ ὕδωρ]" (*Barn.* 11.8; cf. Acts 8:36).[8] He further states, "While we descend into the water [καταβαίνομεν εἰς τὸ ὕδωρ] laden with sins and dirt, we rise up [ἀναβαίνω] bearing fruit in our heart" (11.11). Everett Ferguson contends that these two portions clearly indicate total immersion as the mode of baptism. He also suggests that the early church conducted the baptismal rite outdoors in flowing water (cf. the epistle's reference to a flowing river, "Καὶ ἦν ποταμὸς ἕλκων ἐκ δεξιῶν," *Barn.* 11.10). Thus, the relevant evidence lends credence to the practice of immersion rather than infusion or aspersion, which would not necessarily demand the use of running water.[9] Phillip Schaff confirms the latter point and states that the early church practiced baptism "on streams in the open air."[10]

Nevertheless, theologians must use caution when speculating about the text's authorial intent. Baptizing outside in flowing water was both accessible and free. Such ceremonies were optimal for a growing religious movement that was not yet conventional or state sponsored. At this point, both partial and total immersions were still possible since the text only identifies the petitioner's presence in water. It does not describe whether the early church submerged the new convert's entire body or only partially drenched it.

The Shepherd of Hermas (ca. AD 115-160)[11]

The *Shepherd of Hermas* first mentions baptism by alluding to an open body of liquid, apparently ample enough for the catechumen "to roll into the water [κυλισθῆναι εἰς τὸ ὕδωρ]" (*Herm. Vis.* 3.7.3).[12] The use of a large area to conduct baptisms also indicates that the ceremony took place outside. While outdoor baptisms are ideal for immersion practices, they do not necessarily require a total submersion of the candidate. In fact, the location of the ceremony must not be viewed as dictating any one particular mode of baptism. Rather, the use of public water supplies may simply indicate the resourcefulness of a fledgling and disadvantaged sect.

---

[8] All Greek and English texts of *Barnabas* appear in Michael William Holmes, ed., *The Apostolic Fathers: Greek Texts and English Translations of Their Writings*, 2nd ed., trans. J. B. Lightfoot and J. R. Harmer (Grand Rapids, MI: Baker Books, 1999), 304-7.

[9] Everett Ferguson, "Christian and Jewish Baptism According to the *Epistle of Barnabas*," in *Dimensions of Baptism: Biblical and Theological Studies*, ed. Stanley E. Porter and Anthony R. Cross (New York: Sheffield Academic Press, 2002), 221-22.

[10] Philip Schaff, "§ 108. Baptisteries, Grave-Chapels, and Crypts," in *History of the Christian Church*, vol. 3, *The Middle Ages* (1910; repr., Grand Rapids, MI: William B. Eerdmans Publishing Company, 1994), 558.

[11] Norman Geisler and William Nix state that the *Shepherd of Hermas* could be as early as AD 115 (Norman L. Geisler and William E. Nix, *A General Introduction to the Bible*, Revised and Expanded [Chicago: Moody Press, 1996], 424). However, Alexander Roberts, James Donaldson, and A. Coxe believe it to be as late as AD 160 (Alexander Roberts, James Donaldson, and A. Cleveland Coxe, eds., "The Pastor of Hermas," in *The Ante-Nicene Fathers: The Writings of the Fathers Down to A.D. 325*, vol. 2, *Fathers of the Second Century* [1885; repr., Peabody, MA: Hendrickson Publishers, 2004], 3).

[12] All Greek and English texts of *Shepherd* appear in Holmes, 358-59, 382-83.

The most allusive feature in Hermas' work appears in his second book of *Mandates*, which reads, "There is no other repentance than that which takes place, when we descended into the water [ὅτε εἰς ὕδωρ κατέβημεν] and received remission of our former sins" (*Herm. Mand.* 4.3.1). The description of descending (καταβαίνω) into the water, similar to *Barnabas*, indicates immersion as the primary mode of baptism (cf. Hermas' description of ascending through water in order to be made alive, "εἶχον δι' ὕδατος ἀναβῆναι, ἵνα ζωοποιηθῶσιν," *Herm. Sim.* 9.16.2). However, the terminology is ambiguous and can only eliminate aspersion and affusion as the prescribed mode of baptism.

The Didache (ca. AD 60-150)[13]

The *Didache* is the most important document regarding baptism in the subapostolic era because it gives a clearly defined outline concerning the procedures for baptism. It instructs Christians to baptize in running water (lit. "living water" [ὕδωρ ζῶν], *Did.* 7.1-2; cf. John 4:10), which at least confirms the practice of partial immersion. The text makes a distinction between immersion and affusion in the ensuing passage, "But if you have no running water, then baptize in some other water; and if you are not able to baptize in cold [ψυχρῷ] water, then do so in warm [θερμῷ]. But if you have neither, then pour water on the head three times [ἔκχεον εἰς τὴν κεφαλὴν τρὶς ὕδωρ] 'in the name of Father and Son and Holy Spirit'" (*Did.* 7.2-3).[14]

The identification of cold liquid may reference outdoor locations, such as using the cold water from lakes and ponds. Ferguson notes that the imperative for triple pouring on the candidate's head could indicate the practice of submerging the body three times. If this is the case, then affusion may have been a substitute for submersion in an attempt to cover the entire body with water. Similarly, the allowance of perfusion (pouring water over the head) may have been to imitate the naturally flowing water commonly present in ideal outdoor locations.[15] Unfortunately, the text of the *Didache* only indicates immersion in running water. It does not mention any specific acts of pouring or submerging with regards to the preferred method.

Nonetheless, the most noteworthy feature is the insignificance given to the mode of baptism. The *Didache* favors the catechumen's presence in water. However, if immersion was not possible, then infusion was acceptable, as well. William BeVier remarks, "The concept appears to be that any mode can be used, just so water is applied. The immersionists can well point out that their mode seems to have first choice….and indeed the very tone of the *Didache* seems to allow a great amount of freedom as to mode and amount of water used."[16] Ferguson notes that this is not the only example of a permissible substitute.[17] The only

---

[13] Geisler and Nix date the *Didache* to the first half of the second century, between AD 120 and 150 (Geisler and Nix, 424). Michael Holmes, on the other hand, believes it to be as early as the latter half of the first century, AD 60-100 (Holmes, 247-48).

[14] All Greek and English texts of the *Didache* appear in Holmes, 258-59.

[15] Ferguson, *Baptism in the Early Church*, 203-5.

[16] William A. BeVier, "Water Baptism in the Ancient Church Part I," *Bibliotheca Sacra* 116, no. 462 (April 1959): 142.

[17] Everett Ferguson, "Baptism from The Second to The Fourth Century," *Restoration Quarterly* 1, no. 4 (Winter 1957): 186-88.

required practice was the triune confession of faith in the name of the Father, the Son, and the Holy Spirit (7.1, 3).

The *Didache* also indicates the practicality of baptism in the early Christian church. It answers how Christians were to baptize in locations that lack access to an adequate water supply. It also indirectly addresses the issue of baptizing new converts in different seasons when rivers and lakes are frozen or when droughts have dried the streams. The early church appeared to be conscientious of the possibility of a deficiency in flowing water. The *Didache* allows for more practical methods, such as pouring liquid rather than require immersing someone in the wilderness. This conscious effort by the early church indicates that they were more concerned with the triune confession of faith than they were with the ritual itself.

Ante-Nicene Writings (AD 150-300)

The writings of the ante-Nicene era also demonstrate that the early church prioritized immersion as the favored mode of baptism. However, this period also tended to disregard the necessity of baptizing outside. The writings clearly define trine immersion (baptizing a petitioner three times) as a common mode of baptism, but most descriptions are not explicit whether baptism involved total or partial immersion. Some of the writings argue that affusion and aspersion are sufficient in the case of clinical baptisms, such as sickbed conversions and impending deaths. Interestingly, these writings also indicate that the mode of baptism was irrelevant to the early church.

Justin Martyr (d. ca. AD 165)[18]

Justin Martyr, in a short introduction to baptism in his *First Apology*, sought to "relate the manner in which we [Christians] dedicated ourselves to God" (*1 Apol.* 61.1).[19] He mentioned that the baptismal candidates approached a large body of water, which likely confirms the use of outdoor baptisms.[20] Again, using wilderness locations was ideal for immersion practices and would not always be necessary for affusion or aspersion. The text continues to suggest immersion when Justin compared baptism to a total washing of the body, "Those who enter their temples … they cause them also to wash themselves entirely [λούεσθαι]" (62.1).[21] In this particular example, Justin described other religious practices that imitated the church's baptismal rite. It is likely that Justin was acknowledging the mode of immersion. However, it is not certain whether he meant total submersion or partial immersion since both wash the entire body.

In his *Dialogue with Trypho*, Justin may have alluded to submersion when he described the depraved state of the baptismal candidates as they are "plunged" or "dipped" (βεβαπτισμένους) in water. The use of this particular Greek inflection resembles the form used in other ancient texts, which describe a person being overwhelmed by various magical, physical, or mental influences. The verb's base root (βάπτω) often signifies the total submersion of an object

---

[18] James Eckman dates Justin Martyr's execution to approximately AD 165 (James P. Eckman, *Exploring Church History* [Wheaton, IL: Crossway Books, 2002], 24-25).

[19] All English translations of Justin Martyr's work appear in Roberts, Donaldson, and Coxe, vol. 1, *The Apostolic Fathers, Justin Martyr, Irenaeus*, 183-84, 242.

[20] Ferguson, *Baptism in the Early Church*, 239.

[21] Roberts, Donaldson, and Coxe, 1:184. All Greek texts of Justin Martyr's work appear in Ferguson, *Baptism in the Early Church*, 241-43.

under water, similar to a ship sinking or a person drowning. However, the word is also applied to "dipping" only a part of the body in liquid (cf. Luke 16:24; John 13:26; Rev. 19:13).[22]

Thus, Justin's use of the word does not necessitate total submersion, but it is likely that the entire body is overwhelmed with water during the baptismal rite, "By purifying [us] with water, [Jesus] has redeemed us, though plunged [βεβαπτισμένους] in the direst offences which we have committed, and has made [us] a house of prayer and adoration" (*Dial.* 86.6).[23] Ferguson ascribes submersion to this statement and paraphrases it accordingly, "Those plunged in sins are now plunged in the water that purifies from sins."[24] When connected to the pervasiveness of human depravity, being "plunged" in water likely references the practice of total submersion.

The Hippolytan Community (Third Century AD)

Recent examinations of the literary corpus generally attributed to the Roman presbyter Hippolytus (ca. AD 170-236) have cast doubt on whether he was the actual author of the so-called Hippolytan texts. Allen Brent suggests that several ancient writings, such as the *Apostolic Tradition*, may have originated from a Hippolytan community, which shared Hippolytus' antagonistic beliefs in the late second and early third centuries.[25] In order to identify literary references to baptism, this research will treat the Hippolytan texts as a compilation of writings that eventually endured in a Roman community around the third century.[26]

The *Apostolic Tradition* is the most detailed and comprehensive description of the early church's catechesis.[27] Again, the text indicates the prevalence of running water when its author instructed liquid to flow into a baptismal pool. Ferguson notes that differing versions of the *Apostolic Tradition* give an exception to the type of water that can be used, "The Arabic and Ethiopic versions state that in the absence of water to flow into the place of baptism, any water that can be found is to be poured into the font" (*Trad. ap.* 21.1-2).[28] As before, the

---

[22] See Albrecht Oepke, "βάπτω," in *Theological Dictionary of the New Testament*, ed. Gerhard Kittel and Gerhard Friedrich, trans. Geoffrey W. Bromiley (Grand Rapids, MI: William B. Eerdmans Publishing Company, 1964), 1:529-30.

[23] Roberts, Donaldson, and Coxe, 1:242.

[24] Ferguson, *Baptism in the Early Church*, 243.

[25] Allen Brent, *Hippolytus and the Roman Church in the Third Century: Communities in Tension before the Emergence of a Monarch-Bishop* (Leiden: E. J. Brill, 1995), ch. 3.

[26] For a survey of the different perspectives, including supports and complications with the traditional assignments, see Alistair Stewart-Sykes, *On the Apostolic Tradition: An English Version with Introduction and Commentary*, Popular Patristics Series 22 (Yonkers, NY: St. Vladimir's Seminary Press, 2001), 49-50; Paul F. Bradshaw, Maxwell E. Johnson, and L. Edward Phillips, *The Apostolic Tradition: A Commentary*, Hermeneia: A Critical and Historical Commentary on the Bible (Minneapolis: Fortress Press, 2002), 14; and John F. Baldovin "Hippolytus and the Apostolic Tradition: Recent Research and Commentary," *Theological Studies* 64, no. 3 (September 2003): 520-42.

[27] A "catechesis" is the instruction, preparation, and administration of baptism. See Geoffrey Wainwright, "Baptism," in *The Encyclopedia of Christianity*, ed. Erwin Fahlbusch and Geoffrey William Bromiley (Grand Rapids, MI: William B. Eerdmans Publishing Company, 1999), 1:186.

[28] Ferguson, *Baptism in the Early Church*, 330. Together with the Sahidic (S) version, the Arabic (A) and Ethiopic (E) texts state, "…*utere aquam quam invenis* (S) *fundat aquam quam invenit* (A) *fundat aquam*

flow of water into the pool can suggest both total and partial immersion. It is likely to indicate partial immersion if the stream was used to pour water on the petitioner's head. Of course, the flow of water may not have been used to drench the candidate at all and could have been for purely aesthetic or symbolic purposes.

The *Apostolic Tradition* further indicates immersion practices when describing the catechumen's presence in a pool of water:

> Then, after these things, let him give him over to the presbyter who baptizes, and let the candidates stand in the water, naked, a deacon going with them likewise. *And when he who is being baptized goes down into the water (Cum ergo descendit qui baptizatur in aquam)*, he who baptizes him, putting his hand on him, shall say thus: Dost thou believe in God, the Father Almighty? And he who is being baptized shall say: I believe. Then holding his hand placed on his head, he shall baptize him once. And then he shall say: Dost thou believe in Christ Jesus, the Son of God, who was born of the Holy Ghost of the Virgin Mary, and was crucified under Pontius Pilate, and was dead and buried, and rose again the third day, alive from the dead, and ascended into heaven, and sat at the right hand of the Father, and will come to judge the quick and the dead? And when he says: I believe, he is baptized again. And again he shall say: Dost thou believe in [the] Holy Ghost, and the holy church, and the resurrection of the flesh? He who is being baptized shall say accordingly: I believe, and so he is baptized a third time. *And afterward, when he has come up [out of the water] (Et postea cum ascenderit ex aqua)*, he is anointed by the presbyter with the oil of thanksgiving, the presbyter saying: I anoint thee with holy oil in the name of Jesus Christ. And so each one, after drying himself, is immediately clothed, and then is brought into the church. (*Trad. ap.* 21.11-20)[29]

There are several striking points about this text. First, the document indicates the use of trine immersion, baptizing the catechumen after each confession of faith. Second, placing a hand on the head preceded the act of baptizing. Ferguson argues, "The hand on the head was functional in the immersions," meaning the baptizer used his hand to plunge the candidate's body under water.[30] Third, the text describes the act of entering a pool of water nude, ascending from the water, and the need to dry the body. Ferguson concludes that nudity, hands on the head, and the depiction of a significant amount of water is clear evidence for submersion.[31]

Despite these assertions, Ferguson's conclusion is not the only explanation. If the catechumen were partially submerged and had water poured over their head, then nudity would be preferred to drenching the candidate's clothes, and it would also require drying the

---

hauriendo eam (E)." For a critical examination of the *Apostolic Tradition* 21, see Dom Bernard Botte, *La tradition apostolique de saint Hippolyte: Essai de reconstitution* (Münster, Germany: Aschendorffsche, 1963), 44-59.

[29] The English translation appears in Burton Scott Easton, trans., *The Apostolic Tradition of Hippolytus: Translated into English with Introduction and Notes* (1934; repr., Hamden, CT: Archon Books, 1962), 46-47; brackets appear in the original with emphasis added to the English translation. The Latin text appears in the Testamentum Domini (T), Latin (L), and Bohairic (B) versions of the *Apostolic Tradition* (Botte, 48-51).

[30] Ferguson, *Baptism in the Early Church*, 331.

[31] Ferguson, "Baptism from The Second to The Fourth Century," 197.

body. Likewise, the text indicates that the laying on of hands was part of the confession process. Hands on the head do not preclude the possibility of perfusion. The text simply does not state that the baptizer guided the person's head under water. It could also have alluded to the act of guiding someone's head under a fountain, since streams are mentioned in the preceding passage.

Finally, the text does not specify the amount of water in the baptismal font. It merely indicates the presence of liquid. Strikingly, the Hippolytan community references a small amount of water elsewhere. In *On the Holy Theophany*, the Hippolytan community described the irony of a small amount of water being used at Jesus' baptism, "How should the boundless River that makes glad the city of God have been dipped in a little water [ἐν ὀλίγῳ ὕδατι ἐλούετο]! The illimitable Spring that bears life to all men, and has no end, was covered by poor and temporary waters [πενιχρῶν καὶ προσκαίρων ὑδάτων ἐκαλύπτετο]" (*Serm. Theoph.* 2)![32]

The Hippolytan Community also provides another fascinating detail about Jesus' baptism that may expound on the ceremony. The community wrote, "He [Jesus] bent His head to be baptized by John [ἔκλινεν τὴν κεφαλὴν αὐτοῦ βαπτισθῆναι ὑπὸ Ἰωάννου]" (*Serm. Theoph.* 4).[33] This text may suggest what Ferguson calls the "Dunkers' method," which involves the catechumen kneeling in water and bending forward to complete the submersion process.[34] He expressly rejects the idea that the ancient church practiced the same method of baptism as performed by "some modern religious groups of laying the person back horizontally."[35] In contrast to this theory, however, the text could just as easily be describing Christ's humility during His baptism. At this point, immersion is certain, but total submersion is still conjectural.

More significantly, however, the Hippolytan writings emphasize the faith and character of the catechumen rather than the mode of baptism. Prior to initiation, the church required that candidates provide witnesses to their good conduct (*Trad. ap.* 15), attend several years of instruction (17), and be subject to an examination of their virtuous living (20). Early Christians did not consider the catechumen as part of the church until evidence of their faith and character were assured prior to the act of baptism (18-19). Thus, the community was more interested in the transformation of the person than they were with ritualistic practices. This may also explain why the various writings are often ambiguous in their descriptions and terminology of the ceremony.

Clement of Alexandria (b. ca. AD 150)[36]

Clement of Alexandria's writings describe baptism as a dipping process, which hints at immersion, "Let us quench the fiery darts of the evil one with the moistened sword-points, those that have been dipped in water by the Word [ὑπὸ τοῦ λόγου βεβαμμέναις]" (*Protr.* XI).[37] He painted the clearest picture of immersion when duplicating Hermas' description of descending into (καταβαίνω) and ascending out of (ἀναβαίνω) the water, "They descended

---

[32] The English translation appears in Roberts, Donaldson, and Coxe, eds., vol. 5, *Hippolytus, Cyprian, Caius, Novatian, Appendix*, 235. The Greek text appears in Jacques-Paul Migne, ed., "Sermo in sancta theophania," in *Patrologiae cursus completus: Series graeca* (Paris: 1857), 10:853.

[33] Roberts, Donaldson, and Coxe, 5:235; Migne, 10:856.

[34] Ferguson, "Baptism from The Second to The Fourth Century," 197.

[35] Ferguson, *Baptism in the Early Church*, 850.

therefore into the water with them and again ascended (κατέβησαν οὖν μετ' αὐτῶν εἰς τὸ ὕδωρ καὶ πάλιν ἀνέβησαν)" (*Strom.* 6.6; cf. *Herm. Sim.* 9.16.6).[38] Much like the other writings, however, either total or partial immersion can be seen as the preferred method. While the "dipping" terminology may suggest submersion, it is just as likely that Clement was referring to plunging only a part of the body when he compared the person to "moistened sword-points" rather than to a fully soaked sword (cf. Luke 16:24).

Tertullian (ca. AD 196-212)[39]

Tertullian is the second most prolific writer regarding baptism in the ante-Nicene era. Tertullian expressed a lack of concern over where and how baptism took place, which suggests the early church was more concerned with practicality issues than ritualistic processes. He wrote, "Consequently *it makes no matter* whether one is washed in the sea or in a pond, a river or a fountain, a cistern or a tub [*ideoque nulla distinctio est mari quis an stagno, flumine an fonte, lacu an alveo diluatur*]....Therefore, in consequence of that ancient original privilege, *all waters* [*omnes aquae*], when God is invoked, acquire the sacred significance of conveying sanctity" (*Bapt.* 4).[40] By lending support for various locations, Tertullian may have accepted multiple modes of baptism. For instance, a "sea," "pond," and "river" are ideal for submersion. A "fountain" is useful in partial immersions, where candidates stand in the water and drench their heads. A "cistern" and a "tub" could be used for both affusion and aspersion practices, especially if candidates stood outside a trough and had water poured or splashed on them.

Tertullian also provides a fascinating description of the petitioners bending their knee in preparation for the baptismal ceremony, "Those who are at the point of entering upon baptism ought to pray, with frequent prayers, fastings, [and] bendings of the knee [*geniculationibus et pervigiliis*]" (*Bapt.* 20).[41] Though the statement is possibly an allusion to prayer, it is striking that "bendings of the knee" is listed alongside "frequent prayers," which would make the phrase an odd tautological inference. Rather, bending down may suggest the practice of dunking a candidate's head under water (the "Dunkers' method") or kneeling before an altar.

Regardless, he does mention that immersion was the standard mode of baptism. "When we are going to enter [*adituri*; lit. approach, visit] the water, but a little before, in the presence

---

[36] T. E. Page et al. date Clement of Alexandria's birth to AD 150 and proscribe a late second century period to his teaching ministry (T. E. Page et al., eds., *Clement of Alexandria*, trans. George William Butterworth Loeb Classical Library [1919; repr., Cambridge, MA: Harvard University Press, 1960], xi).

[37] The Greek and English texts appear in Page et al., 248-49.

[38] The English and Greek texts of *Stromateis* 6.6 appear in Schaff, "§ 168. Hermas," in *History of the Christian Church*, vol. 2, *Ante-Nicene Christianity*, 685n1284; italics added to Schaff's Greek text.

[39] Christoph Markschies dates Tertullian's writing period to AD 196-212, (Christoph Markschies, "Tertullian" in *The Encyclopedia of Christianity*, ed. Erwin Fahlbusch, trans. Geoffrey W. Bromiley [Grand Rapids, MI: William B. Eerdmans Publishing Company, 2008], 5:345).

[40] The English and Latin texts appear in Ernest Evans, *Tertullian's Homily on Baptism: The Text Edited with an Introduction, Translation and Commentary* (London: SPCK Publishing, 1964), 10-11; emphasis added to the English translation.

[41] Ibid., 40-41.

of the congregation and under the hand of the president [*sub antistitis manu*]....we are thrice immersed, making a somewhat ampler pledge than the Lord has appointed in the Gospel [*Dehinc ter mergitamur amplius aliquid respondentes quam Dominus in Evangelio determinavit*]" (*Cor.* 3).[42] Here, Tertullian stated that immersion (*mergitamur*, lit. dip, plunge, sink, drown, bury, overwhelm) occurred three times, though he acknowledged that this was not prescribed in the New Testament. He further states elsewhere, "And indeed it is not once only, but three times, that we are immersed into the Three Persons, at each several mention of Their names [*nam nec semel sed ter, ad singula nomina in personas singulas, tinguimur*]" (*Prax.* 26).[43]

In a separate text, Tertullian explicitly depicts baptism as a dipping or sinking motion, "Just as in the baptism itself there is an act that touches the flesh, that we are immersed [*mergimur*] in water, but a spiritual effect, that we are set free from sins [*quomodo et ipsius baptismi carnalis actus quod in aqua mergimur, spiritalis effectus quod delictis liberamur*]" (*Bapt.* 7).[44] Sinking has the potential of alluding to covering the body completely with water in one single motion. Tertullian also contrasts the practice of immersion to aspersion when he wrote, "For who will grant to you, a man of so faithless repentance, one single sprinkling of any water whatever [*Quis enim tibi tam infidae paenitentiae viro, asperginem unam cuiuslibet aquae commodabit?*]" (*Paen.* 6)?[45] Ferguson paraphrases Tertullian's contention, "If you do not genuinely repent, no one will give you even a sprinkling, much less an immersion."[46]

Tertullian further states, "A man is sent down into the water [*homo in aqua demissus*], is washed to the accompaniment of very few words, and comes up little or no cleaner than he was [*non multo vel nihilo mundior resurgit*], his attainment to eternity is regarded as beyond belief" (*Bapt.* 2).[47] Tertullian views the baptismal process as scarcely cleaning the baptizee, possibly suggesting a deficient amount of water to properly bathe someone. However, the action of being lowered into the water (*demissus*; lit. drop, let fall, sink) likely suggests the act of submerging in liquid. What is certain is that some form of immersion, rather than sprinkling or pouring, is the preferred mode of baptism according to Tertullian.

Laurence Stookey comments that partial immersion, rather than total submersion, is still highly probable (i.e. the candidate "dips" his body into the water and is then covered with more liquid). The debate arises over specific baptismal terms ("dip," "plunge," etc.). As Stookey remarks, believing that certain terminology had only one meaning in Greek and Latin would be similar to saying "the Lord's Supper" means only an evening meal in English.

---

[42] The English translation appears in Roberts, Donaldson, and Coxe, eds., vol. 3, *Latin Christianity: Its Founder, Tertullian*, 94. The Latin text appears in George Currey, ed., *Tertulliani libri tres: de spectaculis, de idololatria et de corona militis: Three Treatises of Tertullian with English Notes, an Introduction and Indexes* (Cambridge: John W. Parker, 1854), 119-20.

[43] Roberts, Donaldson, and Coxe, 3:623. The Latin text appears in Ernest Evans, *Tertulliani Adversus Praxean Liber: Tertullian's Treatise Against Praxeas* (London: SPCK Publisher, 1948), 123.

[44] Evans, *Tertullian's Homily on Baptism*, 16-17.

[45] Roberts, Donaldson, and Coxe, 3:661. The Latin text appears in Erwin Preuschen, *Tertullian: De paenitentia. De pudicitia*, Sammlung ausgewählter kirchen- und dogmengeschichtlicher quellenschriften (Freiberg, Germany: J. C. B. Mohr, 1891), 9.

[46] Ferguson, *Baptism in the Early Church*, 341.

[47] Evans, *Tertullian's Homily on Baptism*, 4-5. Cf. the somewhat misleading translation by Roberts, Donaldson, and Coxe, 3:669, "A man is *dipped* in water, and amid the utterance of some few words, is *sprinkled*, and then rises again;" emphasis added to the latter's translation.

He writes, "If the word for baptism can mean nothing except [total] immersion, the references from Peter and Paul make no sense [in 1 Cor. 10:2; 1 Pet. 3:20-21; cf. Luke 11:38]."[48] Nevertheless, Stookey's desire to implement semantic domains to the terminology cannot adequately explain Tertullian's ritual contrasts that try to avoid merely pouring or sprinkling water on the catechumen.

As far as who could perform the ceremony, Tertullian again favors one method but appears to ultimately view it as inconsequential, "Of giving it [baptism], the chief priest (who is the bishop) has the right: in the next place, the presbyters and deacons....Beside these, even laymen have the right; for what is equally received can be equally given" (*Bapt.* 17).[49] Tertullian required that baptism be performed with the authority of the church but, like his view on where and how, was not overly dogmatic. He even viewed the time of baptism as irrelevant, "However, *every* day is the Lord's; every hour, every time, is apt for baptism" (ibid.).[50] If Tertullian was unconcerned about who conducted baptism and when and where it took place, then perhaps he was equally unconcerned about the method, as well. This is especially evident when he acknowledges trine immersion as unscriptural yet still an acceptable practice (*Cor.* 3).

Cyprian (ca. AD 256)[51]

Cyprian wrote his later letters in reaction to the controversy of rebaptizing former Christian schismatics who once followed a rival presbyter named Novatian. In his writings, he referenced the baptismal procedures of this heretical movement as a dipping method, "They who have been dipped [*tincti*; lit. dip, soak] by heretics ought not to be baptized when they come to us" (*Ep.* 70.1).[52] Cyprian hints that the heretical groups utilized the same baptismal procedures as the official church (cf. *Ep.* 75.7). Once again, being "dipped" easily indicates immersion of the candidate. As before, however, the terminology can indicate both submersion and partial immersion of the body since "dipped" requires only that the catechumen be present in water.

Cyprian confirms the practice of immersion when he identifies a difference between standard baptism and the practice of clinical baptism, which was conducted by affusion or aspersion. "Nor ought it to trouble any one that sick people seem to be sprinkled [*aspargi*; lit. splatter, splash] or affused [*perfundi*; lit. pour over, bathe], when they obtain the Lord's grace" (*Ep.* 75.12).[53] Cyprian systematically defended affusion and aspersion in his letter and

---

[48] Laurence Hull Stookey, "Baptism," in *Eerdmans Dictionary of the Bible*, ed. David Noel Freedman, Allen C. Myers and Astrid B. Beck (Grand Rapids, MI: William B. Eerdmans Publishing Company, 2000), 148.
[49] Roberts, Donaldson, and Coxe, 3:677.
[50] Ibid., 3:678; italics in original.
[51] Francine Cardman dates Cyprian's letters (#69-75) to after the council meetings at Carthage in AD 256 (Francine Cardman, "Cyprian of Carthage," in *The Encyclopedia of Christianity*, ed. Erwin Fahlbusch and Geoffrey William Bromiley [Grand Rapids, MI: William B. Eerdmans Publishing Company, 1999], 1:764).
[52] Roberts, Donaldson, and Coxe, 5:377. Cyprian used the Latin *tinguo* and *tinctio* exclusively for heretical baptisms (see Ferguson, *Baptism in the Early Church*, 353n15).
[53] Roberts, Donaldson, and Coxe, 5:401; cf. *Ep.* 75.13-16. The Latin text appears in Ferguson, *Baptism in the Early Church*, 355.

asserted that all modes of baptism have the same meaning. Although he allows for sickbed baptisms, immersion was still the preferred mode in routine circumstances. Ferguson comments, "The objectors to sickbed baptism addressed in this passage based their concerns on its being administered by pouring (or sprinkling) rather than being a complete washing."[54] For Cyprian, it did not matter the amount of water used in baptism since he believed that the Holy Spirit was poured without limits (*Ep.* 75.13-14; cf. John 3:34). BeVier comments, "[Cyprian] made mode a matter of minor importance, provided faith was present in the recipient and ministrant."[55] In the end, Cyprian's writings demonstrate that the early church was sensitive to practical issues involving the infirm and handicap. Adhering to a particular mode of baptism was not the early church's primary focus.

Conclusions Regarding the Ancient Writings

Of the three subapostolic writings included in this report, all three testify that baptism took place outside in running water. This is most ideal for immersion practices and may indicate the candidate's presence in a body of water. *Barnabas* and *Hermas* both describe the catechumen descending into and ascending out of water while the *Didache* distinguishes between being in the water and having water poured over the head. Though immersion is recognized, all three allow for the possibility of total or partial immersion as the primary mode.

There were five authors in the ante-Nicene period that describe the mode of baptism. Two describe the presence of flowing water but only one (Tertullian) explicitly describes an outside scene. At this point in church history, baptism has generally moved indoors. Again, all five indicate at least partial immersion as the primary method, but the terminology and context strongly hint at submersion. In all five writings, the practice of baptism may have involved either total or partial immersion.

Two collections of writings (the Hippolytan community and Tertullian) may allude to Ferguson's "Dunkers' method," which expected the catechumen to kneel or bend forward in order to be completely submerged in water. Ferguson uses this theory to account for most of the ancient church's baptismal ceremonies and even extends his theory to the use of baptisteries later in church history. While admitting that many of the baptismal fonts are too small for a horizontal submersion, Ferguson rationalizes his theory by explaining that outdoor water sources and baptismal fonts are too large to be used solely for pouring water. He writes, "If the baptizand was seated on the interior ledge, was in a kneeling or squatting position, or leaned forward from the waist there was ample space for [a total] immersion."[56]

Unfortunately, there are several practical issues with the "Dunkers' method" that may have diminished its usefulness within the ancient church. To name the most obvious, there is no guarantee that the water in either the outdoor locations or the baptisteries was at a tolerable height for the type of dunking required by Ferguson's theory. The prospect that ancient baptisteries were filled to the brim with water is unlikely. Rather, the earliest baptisteries may have had only one or two feet of liquid, which would have just barely

---

[54] Ferguson, *Baptism in the Early Church*, 356.

[55] William A. BeVier, "Water Baptism in the First Five Centuries Part II: Modes of Water Baptism in the Ancient Church," *Bibliotheca Sacra* 116, no. 463 (July 1959): 237.

[56] Ferguson, *Baptism in the Early Church*, 441.

surpassed the knees of an average person.[57] The impracticality of Ferguson's theory is especially true when considering the elderly, the infirm, and the handicapped, all of whom would have a difficult time bending or kneeling in running water, shallow water, or a confined space within the baptismal font.[58]

Regardless of the potential for submersion, the use of outdoor locations and baptisteries were especially ideal for performing multiple baptisms at the same time. Modern practitioners must recognize that the ancient church did not always baptize single individuals, as is the custom today. It is just as likely that the different baptismal locations were chosen to accommodate simultaneous baptisms of several people. BeVier remarks that because Christianity grew so rapidly and churches conducted baptisms only three or four times a year, "Sometimes hundreds or thousands of converts were baptized at a time" (cf. Tertullian, *Bapt.*, 19).[59] Thus, churches could use one large location to partially immerse several converts simultaneously by perfusion in order to meet the needs of the number of people being baptized.

Nonetheless, the most significant aspect in these writings is the lack of a dogmatic adherence to one particular method. Rather than stress the mode of baptism, they stress the faith and character of the baptizand. While they prefer the catechumen to be present in a pool of water, they also allow for perfusion and infusion in less idyllic circumstances. The *Didache* contends that affusion practices are allowable in less than ideal settings. The Arabic and Ethiopic texts of the *Apostolic Tradition* suggest that the type of water used in baptism was unimportant. Tertullian remarks that it did not matter when, where, or who performed the baptism. He even acknowledges the lack of scriptural support for trine immersion, thereby giving precedence to varying methodologies. Finally, Cyprian argues that the amount of water was unimportant and defended immersion, affusion, and aspersion. Carpenter's study on the formula creeds used during baptismal practices leads him to believe that before the fourth century, there was no established practice for baptism. He concludes, "No writer down to and including Tertullian can be quoted as showing exclusive attachment to one structural form of summary, much less to one exact formula."[60] As BeVier remarks, "No

---

[57] See C. F. Rogers, "Baptism and Christian Archaeology," in *Studia Biblica et Ecclesiastica: Essays Chiefly in Biblical and Patristic Criticism* (Oxford: Clarendon Press, 1903), 5:351. Rogers astutely states concerning one baptistery, contra Ferguson, that the seat ledge may actually demonstrate a shallower water depth, "[The water] was clearly therefore never more than half full, as no one would sit on a seat more than a few inches under the water" (Ibid., 5:350).

[58] The earliest known baptistery is located in the church building at Dura Europos. Clark Hopkins ascribes a date between AD 232 and 256 to this baptismal font (Clark Hopkins, *The Discovery of Dura-Europos*, ed. Bernard Goldman [New Haven, CT: Yale University Press, 1979], 94-96). According to Carl Kraeling, the baptistery is over three feet in depth and over three feet in length. He states that the candidates were clearly meant to enter the font but maintains that the baptistery is not deep enough for a total immersion (Carl H. Kraeling, *The Excavations at Dura-Europos Final Report VIII: Part II The Christian Building*, ed. C. Bradford Welles [New Haven, CT: Yale University Press, 1967], 26-27, 145, 148).

[59] BeVier, "Water Baptism in the First Five Centuries Part II," 235. Ferguson also admits that the early church's propensity to diminish the size of baptismal fonts was in large part due to the declining tradition of baptizing a large number of candidates at once (Ferguson, *Baptism in the Early Church*, 849).

[60] Carpenter, 11:367-77.

uniformity as to mode of water baptism was evident in professing Christendom from the earliest centuries onward."[61]

Application of the Evidence

BeVier makes another studious observation, "[Scholars] seem to give the truth, but never the whole truth, and, therefore very few give testimony to more than one view in respect to mode. Each has his own belief and presents evidence only in favor of that one."[62] Since the writings do not explicitly demand one mode of baptism, there is reason to believe that the method was inconsequential to ancient Christians. The evidence suggests that this ambiguity is because the exact type of baptism was not the early church's primary concern.

In the end, both forms of immersion were practical but not required. Thus, contemporary practitioners can acknowledge one mode of baptism as their preferred method but should not dogmatically disregard the practical aspects of baptizing under less ideal circumstances. There may be cultural, geographical, physiological, or clinical reasons to forego the preferred method and to adapt to the needs of those being baptized. This is especially true in parts of the world where the church does not have access to a sufficient supply of clean water or where health concerns would prevent using water entirely (e.g. new converts who suffer from aquagenic urticarial, aquagenic pruritus, or aquadynia). As G. W. Bromiley contends, "The type of water and circumstances of administration are not important, though it seems necessary that there should be a preaching and confession of Christ as integral parts....Other ceremonies may be used at discretion so long as they are not unscriptural and do not distract from the true action."[63]

---

[61] BeVier, "Water Baptism in the Ancient Church Part I," 144.

[62] Ibid., 137.

[63] G. W. Bromiley, "Baptism," in *Evangelical Dictionary of Theology*, 2nd ed., ed. Walter A. Elwell (Grand Rapids, MI: Baker Academic, 2001), 129.

WHAT'S IN A NAME? RICHARD BAUCKHAM, FIRST-CENTURY PALESTINIAN JEWISH NAMES, AND THE PROTOEVANGELIUM OF JAMES

Michael Strickland*

Few books have received the kind of acclaim from evangelical scholars as Richard Bauckham's *Jesus and the Eyewitnesses*.[1] In the *Journal of the Evangelical Theological Society*, Charles L. Quarles declared it a '*tour de force*' whose "arguments should result in a paradigm shift in Gospel and historical Jesus studies."[2] Ben Witherington surmised that Bauckham had managed to demonstrate that the 'Gospels were written by people who were indeed in touch with vivid eyewitness testimony about events that had been seared into their memory and had left indelible impressions.'[3] However, it would be a mistake to simply label *Eyewitnesses* as an apologetic work, because Bauckham's goal seems to be to challenge overly-critical scholarship, especially form criticism, while acknowledging that "the Gospels come out as a mixture of history and interpretation."[4]

Whether Bauckham's book will indeed succeed in shifting the paradigm of gospel studies will ultimately rest on the strength of his arguments. The purpose of this article is to examine one of the arguments Bauckham offers based upon the record of names in the gospels, specifically to see whether the names given in the gospels *must* be those of eyewitnesses.

Ancient Palestinian Jewish Names (330 BCE – 200 CE)

In chapters three and four, Bauckham argues that the named characters found in the biblical gospels form a realistic catalog of names that would be expected of a first-century Palestinian Jewish community. He is heavily reliant upon the onamistic work of Tal Ilan in her *Lexicon of Jewish Names in Late Antiquity*,[5] which contains the names of as many as three thousand individuals from ancient Palestine during this time.[6] Ilan's data reflect strong tendencies toward certain names, with the nine most popular male names borne by 41.5% of the male population. Bauckham contrasts this with the (admittedly more limited) data from the Jewish Diaspora where only two of the most preferred male names were among the top seven in Palestinian Jewish communities, revealing the differences in naming conventions

---

* Michael Strickland is Assistant Professor of Theology at Amridge University.
[1] The full title is *Jesus and the Eyewitnesses: The Gospels as Eyewitness Testimony* (Grand Rapids: Eerdmans, 2006).
[2] Review of R. Bauckham, *Jesus and the Eyewitnesses*, *JETS* 50 (2007) 617-620, at p.618.
[3] Review of R. Bauckham, *Jesus and the Eyewitnesses*, *BAR* online review at http://www.bib-arch.org/reviews/revieweyewitness.asp].
[4] Stephen J Patterson, Review of R. Bauckham, *Jesus and the Eyewitnesses: The Gospels as Eyewitness Testimony*, Review of Biblical Literature [http://www.bookreviews.org].
[5] *Vol. 1 Palestine 330 BCE-200 CE* (TSAJ 91; Tübingen: Mohr Siebeck, 2002).
[6] Ilan's sources are categorized as: Apocrypha and Pseudepigrapha, Josephus, Greek and Roman Historians, Church Fathers, Rabbinic Literature, Ossuaries, Other Epigraphical material from Jerusalem and Palestine, Epigraphical material from the Diaspora, The Finds of Herodium, and The Judean Desert Document Papyri and Ostraca. See Ilan, 39-45).

outside of Palestine. He posits that the preferences in Palestinian Jewish names reflect a patriotic practice in honor of the Hasmonean reign.[7]

Bauckham's methodology compares the frequency and rank of each of the names catalogued by Ilan and with those in the Gospels and Acts and finds a strong correlation. The most common male name in both Ilan's *Lexicon* and in the Gospels and Acts is Simon, and the name Joseph ranks second in both sources as well. In addition, the names Judas, John and James, which occur for 5 separate characters each in the Gospel and Acts and thus rank third among the male names there, are also frequent in Ilan's *Lexicon*, ranking fourth, fifth, and eleventh respectively.[8] Of all the male names of Palestinian Jews listed in the Gospels,[9] all but three (see below) appear at least 4 times in Ilan's *Lexicon*. Of the Palestinian Jewish male names in Acts, Aeneas and Agabus appear less than four times in Ilan's sources. Bauckham concludes:

> This correspondence is very unlikely to have resulted from addition of names to the traditions, even within Palestinian Jewish Christianity, and could not possibly have resulted from the additions of the names to the traditions outside Jewish Palestine, since the pattern of Jewish name usage in the Diaspora was very different...Again, these features of the New Testament data would be difficult to explain as a result of the random invention of names within Palestinian Jewish Christianity and impossible to explain as the result of such invention outside Jewish Palestine.[10]

But is this conclusion valid? Or do the names, as Christopher Tuckett offered in his critique, simply prove "that the Gospels represent life-*like* stories."[11] Could a writer from outside the Palestinian Jewish Community in the first century invent names that correspond with names from that community?[12] *The Protoevangelium of James* (*PJ*) can serve as a test case.[13]

---

[7] Bauckham, *Eyewitnesses*, 73.

[8] Bauckam's table erroneously states that the name Eros appears in the Gospels and Acts a total of 4 times. See Bauckham, *Eyewitnesses*, 88.

[9] I am using here Bauckham's Table 5 (*Eyewitnesses*, 65-66) where the names of 'Jesus, Old Testament persons, non-human persons, names in the two genealogies of Jesus, public persons, and the Twelve' are excluded.

[10] Bauckham, *Eyewitnesses*, 84.

[11] See *RBL* 12/2007 [www.bookreviews.org/pdf/5650_6184.pdf]. He added the humorous observation that "One does not need to be a literary genius or, for that matter, an exact contemporary of the events concerned, to avoid giving names such as Wayne or Sharon to characters in a story set in nineteenth-century England or in modern-day Japan!"

[12] Quarles, 618, states, "The frequency of common and rare names so closely matches statistical analysis of Palestinian names known from texts and inscriptions from the same era that they could not have been created out of thin air especially outside of Palestine."

[13] My choice of *PJ* has several reasons. First, most of the non-canonical gospels exist in fragmentary form and offer only small portions of gospels. However, there are full texts of the narrative in *PJ* based on many available manuscripts in several languages, the most valuable of which is Papyrus Bodmer 5, a full Greek version of *PJ* from the third century. Second, while *PJ* almost certainly depends on the canonical gospels for inspiration, it also has characters not mentioned in the canonical gospels (as opposed to the Gospel of Thomas), thus offering a name-set independent of the bible. Third, the entire narrative appears to take place in Palestine and thus, one would assume (as Bauckham does for the biblical gospels) that the characters are Palestinian Jews unless otherwise stated. Note that

Most scholars date *PJ* in the mid- to late-second century CE.[14] Details of *PJ* seem to indicate the author's lack of knowledge of Judaism (Mary grows up in the temple) and Palestinian geography (travel *from* Judea to Bethlehem) and strongly indicate an origin outside the Palestinian Jewish Community.[15] Fortunately, Bauckham's opinion on the date and provenance of *PJ* is clear. He writes, "It probably originated in second-century Syria, where its ideas about the virginity of Mary can be paralleled from other texts."[16]

Thus, *PJ* can serve as a good example of material that is not first-hand and is from a non-Palestinian setting. The proper names which appear in *PJ* are:

Name as it appears in PJ[17]	English form in Hock[18]	English form used by Ilan	Rank by Bauckham
Ἰωακεὶμ	Joachim	Yaqim	50
Ῥουβήλ	Reubel	Reuben	39
Ἄννα	Anna	Hannah	13
Ἰουθίνη	Juthine	Judith	16
Μαρία	Mary	Mariam	1
Ζαχαρίας	Zechariah	Zachariah	17
Ἰωσὴφ	Joseph	Joseph	2
Σαμουήλ	Samuel	Samuel	20
Ἐλισάβεδ	Elizabeth	Elisheba	21
Ἄννας	Annas	Hanan	12
Σαλώμη	Salome	Salome	2

---

the spelling *Protoevangelium* and *Protevangelium* are both frequently used in the literature.

[14] Most scholars think that *PJ* was written after the canonical gospels in the late second century: See Tischendorf, *Evangelia Apocrypha* (Leipzig, 1796); Benjamin H. Cowper, *The Apocryphal Gospels, and other Documents, relating to the History of Christ* (London: Frederic Norgate, 1874); Emil de Strycker, *La forme la plus ancienne du Protevangile de Jacques. Recherches sur le Papyrus Bodmer 5 avec une edition du texte grec et une traduction annotee* (Subsidia Hagiographica 33; Brussels: Soc. des Bollandistes, 1961), P.A.van Stempvoort, "The Protevangelium Jacobi, the Sources of Its Theme and Style and Their Bearing on Its Date," in *Studia Evangelica III*, ed. F. Cross. Berlin: Akademie Verlag, 1964), 410-26; H. Smid, *Protevangelium Jacobi: A Commentary* (Assen, Netherlands: Van Gorcum, 1965); J. K. Elliott, The Apocryphal New Testament (Oxford: OUP, 1993); O. Cullmann, "The Protevangelium of James," in E. Hennecke and W. Schneemelcher, eds. *New Testament Apocrypha*, 2 vols., trans. R.M. Wilson (Philadelphia: Westminster, 1991),Vol. 1:370-88; and Ronald Hock, *The Infancy Gospels of James and Thomas: With Introduction, Notes, and Original Text Featuring the New Scholars Version Translations* (Santa Rosa, CA: Polebridge Press, 1995). Contra Otto Bardenhewer, *Patrology: The Lives and Works of the Fathers of the Church* (St. Louis: B. Herder, 1908), 96, who cites Justin Martyr's presumed acquaintance with *PJ* and dates *PJ* in the early decades of the second century. Also contra G. Zervos, "An Early Non-Canonical Annunciation Story," *SBL Seminar Papers 36* (Atlanta: Scholars Press), 664-691, who argues that Luke was dependent upon *PJ*.

[15] But see M. Lowe, "IOUDAIOI of the Apocrypha: A Fresh Approach to the Gospels of James, Pseudo-Thomas, Peter and Nicodemus," *Novum Testamentum* 23 (1981) 56-90, for attempts to answer each of the proposed reasons to claim non-Palestinian and non-Jewish authorship.

[16] R. Bauckham, "Gospels (Apocryphal)", in J. B. Green and S. McKnight (eds.), *Dictionary of Jesus and the Gospels* (Downers Grove, IL: InterVarsity Press), 290.

[17] As taken from Hock.

[18] *Ibid.*

Name as it appears in PJ[17]	English form in Hock[18]	English form used by Ilan	Rank by Bauckham
Ἡρώδης	Herod	Herod	24
Συμεών[19]	Simeon	Simeon	1
Ἰακώβ[20]	James	Jacob	11

Of the names listed above, all but three (Joachim, Rueben and Juthine) are also found in the Gospels and Acts. Four of the names occur in the Gospels and Acts (Anna, Samuel, Annas, and Salome) but refer to different characters than those found in *PJ*. A brief explanation of each of these seven names will be given below. All the other names (Mary, Zechariah, Joseph, Elizabeth, Herod, Simeon, and James) are found in the Gospels and Acts and refer to the same characters in *PJ* and require no explanation.

Joachim

Joachim is introduced at the beginning of the narrative as the wealthy man who will be Mary's father. Bauckham considers *PJ*'s portrayal of Joachim as an aristocratic, elite, master builder an attempt to "provide Jesus with higher social origins than the Gospels imply."[21] According to Ilan,[22] the English form Ἰωακεὶμ, as found in *PJ*, is Yaqim. In Bauckham's table 6[23] Yaqim ranks 50th among Palestinian Jewish names with 7 valid occurrences among Ilan's sources.

Anna

Anna appears at the opening of chapter two, the childless wife of Joachim and soon to be mother of Mary. The Greek name Ἄννα, as found in *PJ*, also appears in Lk 2:36, but there it describes a prophetess who is obviously a different character than the one in *PJ*.

---

[19] In chapter 23 of *PJ*, the priest who takes Zacharias' place after his death is Simeon. His name is variously spelled "Simeon" or "Symeon" in English translations. In Greek, there is little variation in the spelling: P. Bodmer 5 has Συμεων while Vindobonensis Palatinna (VN61) has Συμεῶνα. The Simeon in *PJ* is described as "the one to whom it had been revealed by the Holy Spirit that he would not see death until he saw the messiah in the flesh," being an obvious reference to the Simeon in Lk 2:25-26.

[20] I have included here the name of the purported author of *PJ* because, unlike the Gospels and Acts, the work is not anonymous. Ilan does not include a separate entry for the occurrence of James' name in *PJ*, but does of course document the occurrence of the same character in the NT. It is interesting to note that, if the traditional names typically associated with the canonical gospels are included, they are consistent with Ilan's data. Matthew, or Matthias in Ilan's Lexicon, is the ninth most popular male name and Mark, or Markus, is the sixty-eighth most popular male name Luke would be excluded because he was presumably, according to tradition, not from Palestine. John, or Yohanan in Ilan, is the fifth most popular name (Bauckham, *Eyewitnesses*, 85-87). These characters are, of course, named in the gospels and already factor into Bauckham's results. Perhaps Bauckham would exclude the purported author's name James from this list as he excludes the recipient of Luke, Theophilus (*Eyewitnesses*, 39), presumably because Ilan, 287-88, does not list the occurrence of Theophilus in Luke among her data assuming him to be non-Palestinian.

[21] *Gospel Women: Studies of the Named Women in the Gospels* (Grand Rapids: Eerdmans), 73.

[22] *Lexicon*, 175.

[23] *Eyewitnesses*, 87.

According to Bauckham's Table 7,[24] Anna is the thirteenth most common female name with 4 valid occurrences among Ilan's sources.

Reubel / Reuben

Reubel is Joachim's antagonist who protests the latter's attempted offering to God on the basis of Joachim's childlessness. There is some variation in the manuscripts with this name, but all reflect different forms of the name Reuben. P. Bodmer5 has Ῥουβήλ, which is similar to Josephus' spelling, Ῥουβῆλος, of the Reuben of Genesis.[25] Tischendorf[26] has Ῥουβίμ and de Strycker[27] also lists Ῥουβήν as a variant. Hock offers the English translation of this name as Reubel, though the Roberts-Donaldson[28] translation is Rubim and M.R. James[29] offers Reuben. Ilan considers all these as variations of the English form Rueben.[30] In Bauckham's Table 6,[31] Reuben ranks thirty-ninth among male names with 8 valid occurrences among Ilan's sources.

Juthine / Judith

The most difficult character name in *PJ* is that of Anna's servant (*PJ* 2:3) whose name is uncertain because of variations in the name among manuscripts. The spelling of the name varies considerably, but can be grouped into variations of two names, Juthine and Judith. The standard Greek forms are Ἰουθίνη and Ἰουδιθ. Ilan notes the LXX's Ἰουδείν for the character in Genesis, compared with the form Ἰουδείθ for the name in the apocryphal Judith, which explains the form Ἰουδείθ in *PJ*. She also mentions the occurrence of a similar name, Ἰούθιος, in a papyrus from Egypt. However, Ilan also considers Ἰουθίνη a variant of Ἰουδιθ, though this occurrence does not factor into the valid occurrences of the name because she does not include characters from apocryphal Christian gospels, labeling them "fictitious."[32] In addition, de Strycker considers the name to be a variant of Ἰουδιθ, an attempt by the author of *PJ* to select a Hebrew name, and suggests it is modeled after Esau's wife's name in Gen. 26:34.[33] Therefore it seems best to consider the name Judith, which is listed on Bauckham's Table 7[34] as the sixteenth most popular name with 3 valid occurrences among Ilan's sources. However, see more about the name below in "Conclusions."

---

[24] Ibid., 89.
[25] Josephus, *Antiquities* I 19, II 3. For the Greek, see F. Oberthur (ed.), *Flavii Josephi: Opera Omnia Graece et Latine* (Leipzig, 1787), 101-102. The LXX spelling of this Reuben is Ῥουβήν (Hatch & Redpath Supplement, 130-1).
[26] *Evangelia*, 2.
[27] *La forme*, 163.
[28] *ANCL vol. 16: Apocryphal Gospels, Acts, and Revelations* (Edinburgh: T. & T. Clark), 5.
[29] *The New Testament Apocrypha* (Oxford: Clarendon Press, 1924), 39-41.
[30] *Lexicon*, 209-210.
[31] *Eyewitnesses*, 86.
[32] Ilan, 241.
[33] de Strycker, 312, comments, "Mais l'intention de l'auteur était certainement de donner à la servante un nom hébraïque, comme il le fait pour tous les personnages qu'il ajoute de son cru aux données évangéliques: Joachim et Anne, Annas le scribe, Samuel le fils de Joseph, Salomé."
[34] *Eyewitnesses*, 89.

Annas the scribe

Annas the scribe[35] (ὁ γραμματεὺς) appears at the beginning of the fifteenth chapter of *PJ*, sees the pregnant Mary, and then accuses Joseph of committing a "serious offense" (15.4). An Annas appears in Luke-Acts (Lk 3:2; Ac 4:6) as high priest along with Caiaphas, and in John 18:13 as father-in-law of the high priest Caiaphas. Perhaps the same Annas is meant in *PJ*, but without more evidence it is best to list him as a new character not named in the Gospels and Acts. According to Bauckham's table 6,[36] the name Annas is the twelfth most popular male name with 35 valid occurrences in Ilan's sources.

Samuel

Chapter seventeen of *PJ* mentions a character named Samuel accompanying Joseph, his sons, and Mary on the way to Bethlehem. The name does not appear in every manuscript, though it appears in P Bodmer 5, and Hock includes it in the main text, also mentioning the variants James, Simon and Joseph found among other manuscripts.[37]

Presumably, these were scribal corrections to the supposed error of inserting a new and perhaps wrong character only here in the story.[38] Hock notes that the insertion of "Joseph" for "Samuel" only complicates matters because, though Samuel is said to be following the rest (καὶ ἠκολούθει Σαμουήλ), Joseph is clearly depicted as being ahead of Mary in 17:6 and 17:8. I am inclined to include the name Samuel here because it represents the more difficult reading.[39] Bauckham's table 6[40] shows it to be the twentieth most popular male name with 20 valid occurrences in Ilan's sources.

Salome

A character named Salome appears only once in the Gospels (Mark 15:40, 16:1), but other post-biblical women with that name have received considerable attention from Bauckham.[41] In the twentieth chapter PJ, Salome is a witness to the birth of Jesus, who, while trying to test Mary's virginity, has her hand burned (20:4) and later healed when she touches the child (as she was instructed to do by an angel). This Salome is almost certainly not the disciple of Jesus named in Mark. Bauckham writes,

> The best explanation is that she is Salome the daughter of Joseph, who would naturally have accompanied her father and brothers on their journey to Bethlehem. This is much more plausible than Morton Smith's assumption that she must have been Salome the disciple of Jesus… whom the Protevangelium's readers would hardly

---

[35] Hock, 59, prefers "scholar" to "scribe."

[36] *Eyewitnesses*, 86.

[37] *Infancy*, 63. Bauckham, *Gospel Women*, 230, suggests that "the name of Samuel is most likely a corruption of Simeon."

[38] Hock, 63, notes that James and Simon are listed as brothers of Jesus in Mk 6:3 and Mt 13:55, but not Samuel.

[39] If the name Samuel is excluded, it does not affect the outcome of this investigation since the others found in its place are elsewhere named in *PJ*.

[40] *Eyewitnesses*, 86.

[41] For example, see Bauckham, *Gospel Women*, 225-276 and *Jude, 2 Peter* (WBC 50; Waco, TX: Word Books, 1983), 39-44.

expect to find loitering outside a cave on the road from Jerusalem to Bethlehem at the time of the birth of Jesus.[42]

In Bauckham's Table 7,[43] Salome is the second most popular female name with 58 total valid occurrences in Ilan's sources.

Conclusions vis-à-vis Bauckam's Usage of Names

Of the 14 names appearing in PJ, all 14 are among Ilan's list of popular names assuming that Anna's servant is Judith. There is the possibility that the name Judith or its variant was not original. For example, Gerhard Schneider argues that the name is a traditional Greek name, Euthine, but he chooses to follow de Strycker in the Greek text.[44] If Euthine were original, then the name would not be included among the most popular names according to Ilan.[45] Even so, with only 1 uncommon name out of 14, this compares favorably to the 3 names in Mark's gospel which are not among the most popular names. Of the 20 names in Mark[46] Bartimaeus, Timaeus,[47] and Rufus are not among the top 100 male names. There is one other occurrence of Rufus from an ossuary in Jerusalem which Ilan dates as pre-70 CE.[48] The names Bartimaeus and Timaeus are found only in Mark. Thus, the author of PJ could be said to be at least as talented as the author of Mark at finding believable names for his characters.

This comparison serves to limit the force of Bauckham's argument that the names found in the Gospels suggest the "possibility that many of the named characters were eyewitnesses who not only originated the traditions to which their names are attached but also continued to tell these stories as authoritative guarantors of their traditions."[49] As Tuckett suggested, the names in the Gospels could be simply life-*like*[50] and a different author, from a different time and place, having no acquaintance with the eyewitnesses, could have created realistic names. The author of *PJ* did. This might imply that PJ was based on early traditions from within the Palestinian Christian community, but this only serves to weaken the argument that the Gospels, though possibly composed outside Palestine, offer reliable collections of firsthand accounts from Palestine.

---

[42] *Gospel Women*, 230.

[43] *Eyewitnesses*, 89.

[44] *Evangelia infantiae apocrypha. Apokryphe Kindheitsevangelien* (Freiburg: Herder, 1995), 99. This was also noted in Oliver Ehlen, *Leitbilder und romanhafte Züge in apokryphen Evangelientexten. Untersuchungen zur Motivik and Erzählungsstruktur anhand des Protevanglium Jacobi und der Acta Pilati Graec. B.* (Stuttgart: Franz Steiner Verlag, 2004), 106.

[45] Others who prefer Euthine (with the variant Judith in brackets) are Cullman, 426, and Boyd Daniels, trans., "The Protevangelium of James," in David R. Cartlidge and David L. Dungan, eds. *Documents for the Study of the Gospels* (2nd ed.; Philadelphia: Fortress, 1994), 101-110.

[46] Again, following Bauckham, *Eyewitnesses*, 65 (table 5) where he excludes "Jesus, Old Testament persons, non-human persons, names in the two genealogies of Jesus, public persons, and the Twelve."

[47] Bauckham, *Eyewitnesses*, 65, 79, also counts Timaeus as a separate name because Mark has "Bartimaeus son of Timaeus" in 10:46.

[48] Ilan, 338, n.4.

[49] *Eyewitnesses*, 39.

[50] See note 11 above.

While Bauckham is right that the gospels contain names that would be expected of a first-century Palestinian Jewish community, this fact does not conclusively show that the gospels were a product of that milieu. Of course, this conclusion does not challenge any of Bauckham's more substantial arguments regarding eyewitnesses in the gospels.

BOOK REVIEWS

Cambridge History of Christianity, 9 volumes, Cambridge University Press, 2006-2009.

The *Cambridge History of Christianity* is published in nine volumes. It offers a comprehensive chronological account of the development of Christianity in all its dimensions: theological, intellectual, social, political, regional and global from its beginnings to the present day. The series eschews the notion of Christianity as simply a western European phenomenon and considers it within its global context. Eastern and Coptic Christianity are given full consideration and African, Far Eastern, New World, South Asia and other non-European developments are examined in detail. The relationship between Christianity and other major faiths is examined throughout.

The first volume considers the emergence of Christianity in the Mediterranean world in the first three centuries. Its thirty-two chapters trace this dynamic history from the time of Jesus through to the emergence of imperial Christianity at the beginning of the fourth century. The volume begins with three chapters on the political, social and religious context followed by four on the Jesus movements. Community traditions and self-definition forms the theme of the next seven chapters including an interesting chapter on the Gnostics and this fits well with the next section on regional variations of Christianity. The shaping of Christian theology is examined in five chapters in terms of institutional structures and the development of ideas. The final section moves from the persecutions of the late third century through to imperial patronage and the defining of the Church at Nicaea in 325.

Volume 2 considers the development of Christianity between its recognition under Constantine through to the beginning of the seventh century—what is often seen as the 'golden age' of patristic Christianity. Late Antiquity saw the rapid transformation of Christianity as it enjoyed imperial patronage and eventually became the favoured religion of the empire. These centuries were also ones of religious vibrancy as Christianity impacted on artistic, literary, philosophical, political and cultural developments. Divided into four parts, this volume begins with an examination of the different regional natures of Christianity—western, Germanic and Celtic and Greek—but also looks at its early Asian and East African forms. That Christianity remained contested in late Antiquity is the theme of the second part with a particular focus on its relationships with paganism especially in Egypt, Asia Minor, Italy and North Africa with its relationship with Manichaeism given its own chapter. The third section examines Christian culture and society while the book concludes with twelve chapters on Christian beliefs and practices.

Volume 3 focuses on the vitality and dynamism of all aspects of Christian experience from Late Antiquity through to the First Crusade. It emphasizes the varied expressions of Christianity at both local and global levels. It addresses eastern, Byzantine and western Christianity and explores the encounters and confrontation between Christians and others, especially Jews, Muslims and pagans. The institutional development and life of the church especially the problems of reform and the challenges posed by monasticism place Christianity in the social and political order. Part four is particularly interesting in its discussion of Christianity as lived experience and the place that remedies for sins, sickness and healing, gender, sacrifice, gifts and prayers and the liturgy played in the individual's passage from birth to death. The final part explores books and ideas including heresy, saints' cults and the afterlife.

Volume 4 explores the wide range of institutions, practices and experiences in the lives of European Christians in the later Middle Ages. The opening two parts explore the ways in which the institutional structures of the church changes in the twelfth and thirteenth centuries and how theologians lay the foundations for a Christian world. Part of this process saw the erection of boundaries between Christianity and Christendom in relation to Jews, Islam, heretics and women through, in part the development of more refined notions of heaven, hell and purgatory. Late medieval Europe also saw the development of the Christian life whether like hermits and beguines at the margins of religious life or more aggressively through crusade, holy war and Christian conquest. It also saw the church having to face challenges from within from those who sought a return to the simplicity and purity of the early Church and who regarded its institutional structures as too worldly and its clergy too avaricious. Despite criticism from reformers, the church remained a vital presence in communities whether local or national and the Reformation was by no means inevitable.

Volume 5 examines Eastern Christianity from the Millennium through to the present day covering all the Orthodox Churches (the ecumenical patriarchate of Constantinople and the Russia, Armenian, Ethiopian, Egyptian and Syrian Churches. The central theme is the survival of Orthodoxy against all the odds in its many forms into the modern period. Although there were differences in teachings and experience of its different manifestations, what marked out Orthodoxy was its resilience in the face of alien and hostile political regimes. The last phase of Byzantium appears to have been exceptionally important in this survival providing Orthodoxy with the intellectual, cultural and spiritual reserves to meet these challenges.

Volume 6 presents the history of Christianity from the eve of the Protestant Reformation to the height of Catholic reform. It examines the impact of the permanent schism in Latin Christendom, how the Catholic Church responded to this and the influence of the development of the Orthodox churches. It also examines the relationship between Christianity and non-Christian religions both in Europe and in the global community. It is divided into six parts: the first two deal with the Lutheran Reformation and the second Reformation associated with Zwingli and more importantly John Calvin. Part 3 considers the question of the Catholic renewal and its redefinition at Trent and beyond. This is followed by a section on resolving confessional conflicts with a consideration of the problems of religious toleration, the role of the Mediterranean Inquisitions and Western and Eastern Christianity. Part 5 contains some excellent papers on religion, society and culture extending the theological emphasis of some of the essays to include the visual arts, science and religion and women and religious change. The book ends with an examination of Christianity and other faiths including Judaism, the Andean Christianities, Islam, Hinduism and Buddhism.

Volume 7 explores how three complex movements resulted in a cultural reorientation of Europe and North America and as a consequence the wider world. The Enlightenment transformed views of nature and the human ability to master it. Religious revivalism brought the development of more experiential forms of Christianity. Finally, revolution and the political and social upheavals at the end of the eighteenth century called into question ideas of monarchy by divine right and divinely ordained social structures and promoted more democratic forms of government and notions of human rights and religious toleration. In addition, colonisation and missionaries spread Christianity widely round the globe and responded in different ways to its encounters with other cultures and religious traditions.

Volume 8 takes the story from 1815 through to the outbreak of war in 1914 and is the first treatment of nineteenth-century Christianity as a global phenomenon. The opening chapters consider the ways in which Catholicism and Protestantism responded to the intellectual and social challenges posed by European modernity giving particular attention to the explosion of new voluntary forms of Christianity and the expanding role of women in religious life. This is followed by a section on the complex relationships between the churches and nationalism resulting in fundamental changes it the relationships between church and state. The final section looks at Christianity as a global force as it expanded from its traditional base in Asia and Africa to establish itself in Australasia and how it responded to the challenges and opportunities posed by European imperialism.

Volume 9 examines the twentieth century that saw changes as dramatic as in any period of Christian history. It considers Catholicism, Protestantism and the Independent Churches in all parts of the world as Christianity, really for the first time, becomes a global religion. The first section examines the institutions and movements that can truly be said to have had a global impact especially the Papacy, Pentecostalism and the Ecumenical movement. The second section looks at Christian history in each region of the world and there is an exceptionally valuable study of African Christianity. The final section considers certain themes in their global perspective including changes in worship, relations with Jews and Muslims and the arts, gender and sexuality. This is a volume of incomparable value for those who want to make sense of Christianity in a century when its position was placed under considerable threat in some parts of the globe.

Each of these volumes is edited with considerable skill to ensure that, although there may be differences of emphasis among the different contributors, there is clear coherence. The bibliographies attached to each volume are exhaustive and provide an excellent guide for those who want to take matters further. There is little doubt that this series will become the critical reference point for students and teachers.

Richard Brown
The History Zone
http://richardjohnbr.wordpress.com

***The Cambridge History of Religions in America*, 3 volumes, Stephen J. Stein (editor), Cambridge University Press, 2012.**

The three volumes of *The Cambridge History of Religions in America* examines the development of religious traditions in America from Pre-Columbian times to the present day. They examine the transplantation of religions from different parts of the world to America and consider the development of new religious movements on the continent of North America. The books are a stunning achievement, its essays of high quality and readability and its coverage extensive. Each essay makes good, but not excessive, use of footnotes and has a short list of material for further reading. These go some way to address the needs of those who wish to explore the issues raised in detail but it is unfortunate, though understandable given the size of the volumes, that there is no composite bibliography.

The first volume takes the story from Pre-Columbian times to 1790 and begins with five chapters on the Native American, European and African religious traditions, providing a context for the three volumes. The next section considers the establishment and interplay of religions during the decades of initial discovery and settlement between 1500 and the 1680s. Its six chapters are divided into three of Native American traditions and three on Spanish and French Catholicism and English, Dutch and Swedish Protestantism. This is followed by five chapters on religious patterns in colonial America from the 1680s to the 1730s taking forward the story of Catholicism in New France and in the Caribbean and New Spain and Protestantism in the American colonies. The religious diversity of British America from the 1730s through to the 1790s forms the fourth section and consists of nine chapters exploring, in addition to the impact of evangelicalism, the discontent with Anglicanism and sectarian communities, Judaism, African slave religions and folk magic and religion. American religions in their eighteenth-century international context form the fifth section and examine in particular religion and imperial conflict, religion and the American Revolution and religious nationalism in Spanish America. The volume ends with eight thematic essays that include chapters on religious thought, sacred music, church architecture and religion and race.

The second volume focuses on the period from 1790 through to 1945. This was a period marked by the impact of the religious freedom contained in the United States Constitution resulting in a dramatic expansion of religious diversity within the new nation and with it sectarian controversy and conflict over theological and social issues. This led to the development of quite different patterns of religion in each of its three nations, the United States, Canada and Mexico. The volume opens with four essays on religion in North America considering religious diversity in the 1790s, religion in the Constitutional Tradition, religion and law in British North America and Mexican American faith communities in the Southwest. This is followed by two sections that together chart the development of religious diversity and conflict in the United States with valuable chapters on African Americans, American Indian, Muslim and Asian religion as well as the development of the Protestant and Catholic traditions, Judaism and Eastern Orthodoxy. This was a period of growing religious pluralism with its inevitable social and political tensions particularly evident, for instance, in the chapter on religion and the Civil War. The crisis of modernity and religious responses to modern life and thought forms the next section and explores the response of religion to immigration, the modern city, industrialization, modern science and philosophy as well as fundamentalism. It examines nativism, religiously inspired social reforms, also the First, Second World Wars, and America's religious communities. There are three essays in the section on comparative essays dealing with Canada, Mexico and Caribbean religious history. The volume ends with six essays on 'diverse areas' looking at religion and the media, religion and news, religious music, religion and literature, religion and the courts and religion and American patriotism from 1790 to the present.

The final volume examines the religious situation in the United States from the end of the Second World War in 1945 to the second decade of the twenty-first century and places it within the broader context of North American religious developments. The opening section provides an overview of the post-war religious world with synoptic essays on the United

States, Canada and Mexico as well as on Judaism, suburbanization and religion and Asian religions in the United States. This is followed by a section on controversial issues including a discussion of secularization in American society, the churches and Vietnam, the religious significance of the Civil Rights movement, the new morality and the sexual revolution and the state of Israel. World religions and religious and cultural conflict in the United States are considered in the third and fourth sections of this volume. The final two sections examine new and continuing religious realities in America and four concluding essays. Of especial interest here is a chapter on America and Islam post-9/11.

The *Cambridge History of Religions in America* is comprehensive in its coverage of the critical developments in and conflicts over religion since the beginnings of European settlement. It demonstrates the vibrancy of the religious scene in the pluralistic United States as well as the different religious traditions of Canada and those areas originally settled by Spain. The various essays, well over a hundred across the three volumes, are combative, challenging and indicate the most recent interpretations of the subject. The University Press and all those involved deserve congratulations on what is a massive achievement.

Richard Brown
The History Zone
http://richardjohnbr.wordpress.com

***Ways of Meeting and the Theology of Religions.* By David Cheetham. Aldersgate: Ashgate Publishing, 2013. 224pp.**

Near the end of this latest work by David Cheetham (Univ. of Birmingham), the following quotation emerges from W. Ustorf: "Was it feasible that in this universe all [religious] conflicts could be 'received' and 'resolved' because the opponents would pause in their fight and join the 'third space' the professors themselves were inhabiting?" The query is trenchant and the target is two-fold: (a) academic discourse and (b) how it handles interreligious engagement. For Ustorf, as for many others, religious interaction ought to be firmly grounded in the *practical*, especially in light of religion's ever-increasing significance in our late-modern, globalized communities. But if history is any indication, no conversation is able to more markedly dodge practicality than that which transpires in academia. So the point is well-taken: in a post-9/11 world, where religious traditions routinely collide over sacred geography, textual interpretation, human rights, and radicalism, what can the academic study of interreligious theology really contribute that has *practical* value? If all the theological and hermeneutical gymnastics have only resulted in mere theoretical constructs, one justly wonders what has been accomplished. Religion, after all, is so much more than theory or abstract dogma—it is the cultural and devotional lifeblood of actual human beings, striving after identity and understanding amidst the manifold struggles of contemporary life. It is with this fundamental perspective firmly in hand that Cheetham has produced a work which is both textured in discussion and fascinating in uniqueness. It focuses not on theoretical harmonizations between religious systems, but rather on the cultivation of deep interreligious meetings between people, on wavelengths *besides* that of the expressly theological or dogmatic.

With the same dialogical incisiveness that has characterized his other recent projects (e.g. his fine essays in *Intercultural Theology* (2011) and *Understanding Interreligious Relations* (2013), volumes which he also co-edited), Cheetham sets out on a nuanced quest to "*de-intensify* the debate in the theology of religions and lower the stakes; finding cooler, less claustrophobic spaces for meeting that are not overly weighed down with theological or religious luggage" (2). At first glance, statements like this one, though evocative, may seem to be aiming at something too literal to be helpful or too metaphorical to be understood. However, with requisite clarity, Cheetham unfolds his fascinating suggestions for just what some of these "cooler, less claustrophobic spaces" might look like in the course of interreligious engagement.

Chapter 1 sets its sights on decidely non-theological notions such as good humor and imagination. It is here that Cheetham, after laying his own theoretical cards on the table (e.g., in a comparison between John Hick and Gavin D'Costa, Cheetham finds himself more in alignment with the latter [19]), begins to develop the manner of serious-yet-playful discussion that will become resonant throughout the work. He suggests that even the most philosophical of interreligious discussion can undetake "the task of comparison with good humour" (36), and he directs attention to the fact that it is *inspiration*, arising from the varied religious narratives of the world, which piques our curiosity and drives us to investigation (37). Why should this vital human impulse always be articulated in dry, dessicated, or combative ways? He alludes to further chapters, which will search for comparative spaces that subsist in "a spirit of play rather than a constricted guardedness" (38).

"Tones of Voice" is the topic for Chapter 2, and it is meant to address the key question of *how religious traditions ought to be spoken of* if true encounter is to be facilitated in the midst of diversity. Through a fascinating dual-examination of the philosophical pluralism of Hick and the confessional exclusivity of John Milbank's Radical Orthodoxy, Cheetham highlights how these *second-order* discourses about religion perilously avoid making *real* connections, either with the particular religious textures themselves (Hick) or with the world beyond one's own tradition (Milbank). In contrast to this, Cheetham advocates for an honest, open religious voice that "speaks to the confessional religious imagination in first-order terms" while simultaneously seeking to "reasonably correspond to the broader concerns of the world and nature" (59).

This is, as said, a work predicated on the notion that interreligious involvement ought not be merely theoretical. But Cheetham is under no delusions that his project can proceed with any effectiveness apart from *some interaction* with more theoretical theology. Thus we find the requisite chapter on theology of religions (Chapter 3), but here with a twist. Whereas theology of religions has been seen as the "proper" way for Christian thinking to array itself against the claims of religious others (often by way of the now-classic typology: exclusivism, inclusivism, pluralism), Cheetham critiques such approaches, essentially claiming that because they often derive their typological structures via metaphysical schematizing, they automatically charge all religious encounters with a threatening ultimacy. Rather than seeking to locate all religious expressions in reference to the greatest conceivable ontological depths (salvation, heaven, the "one true God", etc.), Cheetham advocates for "depths between the depths" (79)—appreciation for beauty, shared humor, and enjoyable experiences that exist apart from any moral pay-off (80-84). Such depths are not traditionally theological, but in them Cheetham perceives ways in which those of differing religious sentiments can *meet* over important areas of human life while not having to categorize each other in ultimate terms. The next chapter follows up such notions by articulating an anthropological outlook which draws on the ideas of "plural self" from contemporary psychology, "interior castle" from the mystic Teresa of Avila, and Bonhoeffer's sense of "overabundant freedom" for encountering others. In the midst of this highly textured anthropology, the self comes to be viewed as a "bestowed self" and thus it "enjoys a freedom to be, a gratitude of being loved, a humility to engage with others without the need to anxiously safeguard the self as if it were one's own construction" (115).

Theological planking now in place, Cheetham proceeds into what is definitively the most unique chapters of the work: actual discussions of possible "ways of meeting" which eschew theology of religions ultimacy and which appreciate the manifold freedom of the self-in-encounter (Chapters 5-7). One of the described possibilities consists of meeting within "aesthetic spaces," where playfulness and imagination with the religious other (or in the midst of their artwork, rituals, or sacred spaces) is allowed to generate a "creative interplay of free ideas and feelings" (131). Another possibility of shared space is that of the ethical. Cheetham perceives in ethics "a common language that permits the sharing of concerns separate from religious imperatives[...] a worthy 'distraction' away from the domain of explicitly religious truth-claims" (151). Well aware of the critical heritage of Hans Kung's "global ethic"—deriving from the fact that such pan-religious ethical systems can sometimes neglect the very real religious differences which underlie similar-sounding ethical principles (157)—Cheetham instead advocates not for a "common ethic" but for "*joint-creativity*" amidst religious others in handling moral issues (161).

In his last chapter, Cheetham critically interacts with the recent Scriptural Reasoning movement, wherein adherents of the three Abrahamic faiths are encouraged to meet and read their shared scriptures together (Peter Ochs and David Ford, among others, have been at the spearhead of this venture). Though SR meetings thus far have been primarily academic in nature, Cheetham highlights that "friendships and understandings" have emerged "more than any hermeneutical advancement" (178). It is the sustained meeting and relationship-building that Cheetham finds most attractive here; but he does suggest that SR may seek to include those beyond the Abrahamic religions, and he constructs an interesting case for how this might be done (189-191).

Each chapter pulses with deep scholarly engagement and a masterful parsing of attendant issues. The entire work also has a provisional tone, a real strength given the unique nature of the project which Cheetham is undertaking. If any critique had to be offered, it would be along the lines of further questions that perhaps could have been addressed. One such question would be: How should we understand the *relationship* of these sorts of "less claustrophobic" interreligious meetings to the more ultimate questions of religious truth? Cheetham doesn't really address this specifically, though at times he seems to hope that after the cultivation of relationship in these less threatening spaces, issues of ultimacy might be broached more honestly and effectively. However, this optimistic outlook could be countered by suggesting the very real possibility that questions of ultimacy would be *less likely* to be broached at all in light of successful interreligious meetings in non-ultimate (and thus more comfortable) spaces.

As theology of religions, comparative theology, and intercultural theology pursue myriad important tasks in religious understanding and relations, David Cheetham's latest work shines prominently as an example of creative thinking bolstered by academic astuteness. For any course on interreligious theology or engagement, especially at the graduate level, this text would be sure to spur both discussion and reflection, and I recommend it highly.

Samuel Jacob Youngs
King's College, London

Heavenly Participation: The Weaving of a Sacramental Tapestry. **By Hans Boersma. Eerdmans Publishing, 2011. 224 pp.**

In Hans Boersma's provocative book on the early Christian understanding of a "participatory" cosmos, the J.I. Packer Professor of Theology (Regent College) calls for a *ressourcement* (by which he means rediscovery and application) of the christological worldview that flourished during the first thousand years of church history. Without such a ressourcement of early Christian (patristic) theology, he warns, the divisions in the Body of Christ caused by the 16th century Protestant Reformation will continue to multiply.

These rifts between Christian denominations, which Boersma calls the "tearing" of the garment of Christ, found their source in the theological innovations of the second millennium which overemphasized the autonomy of nature and elevated the Church's monopoly of grace. In time, the role of Christ as Pantocrator (Ruler of All/Sustainer of the World) became obscured behind a naturalism and formalism that secularized the cosmos. When using the term secularization, Boersma speaks of scientific, political, and philosophical epistemologies that seek an understanding of the world apart from the creation and providence of God. As a result of bad theology and the schisms it produced, Christ's bride—the Church—now lives in a "secular" culture where she is divided into some 41,000 denominations. In order to heal the wounds of division, Boersma suggests that we first learn to weep over the theological errors that secularized and divided God's household. Only then, once evangelicals do justice to their past by "regard[ing] the Reformation not as something to be celebrated but as something to be lamented," can the Church begin her recovery of the undivided, participatory world of the early Church Fathers (85).

Heavily influenced by the twentieth century "Nouvelle Théologie" (De Lubac, Daniélou, von Balthasar and Chenu) as well as the major voices of patristic theology (especially Irenaeus, Athanasius, Gregory of Nyssa and Augustine) which inspired them, Boersma's book scours the last eight-hundred years of Christian theology for the ideological roots of secularism that produced the schisms of the Reformation and still haunts Christianity to this day. The rise of secularism, or the "unraveling of the sacramental tapestry," as Boersma calls it, had its source in the medieval "revolt of nature." According to Boersma, a number of developments within the Church contributed to this revolt. Among them, Boersma lists the following: the administrative growth and politicization of the Roman Catholic Church; the rise of Aristotelean naturalism; the tensions posited between scripture and tradition; the separation of nature and the supernatural; and the theology of Scholastics such as John Duns Scotus (who placed philosophical categories above God) and William of Ockham (who denied universals). A combination of these errors, according to Boersma, fostered a worldview in which nature was seen as a semi-autonomous being with a natural teleology distinct from its supernatural teleology found in Christ. While the Protestant Reformation sought to correct "doctrinal issues and abusive practices that certainly needed to be addressed, [it] failed to address appropriately the underlying problems that had given rise to the need for reform" (87). The shortsightedness of the Reformers was caused by some false dichotomies maintained in the theological systems of the 16th century (in the West) which made sharp distinctions between Nature and the Supernatural; Faith and Reason; Heaven and Earth; Scripture and Tradition; and Symbol and Reality. Instead of working to resolve the problem of secularization, these distinctions further perpetuated the secularization of the world and left "the Church" divided in its testimony to non-believers.

It is in light of this secularization that Boersma prescribes participatory, or sacramental, ontology as an antidote to heal the Church. For Boersma, sacramental ontology is not to be understood in the narrow sense of specific rites like those performed by the medieval Church; rather, he looks at the larger narrative of how the "created world point[s] to God as its source and 'point of reference,' but…also subsists or participates in God" (24). While his ontology emphasizes the importance of Baptism and the Eucharist for forming a coherent, Christ-centered worldview, Boersma believes that it is by re-affirming the Protestant belief in the supremacy and continuing lordship of Christ, and expanding the scope of its implications, that we can hope to recover the fullness of the gospel as preached in the early church.

What follows are some concrete examples of how Boersma's theology of participation impacts our understanding of Theology, Tradition, Biblical Interpretation, Philosophical Truth, and the Church.

Theology, for Boersma, should be about initiation "of the community into the divine life of joyous sacramental participation" (179). Humans know God foremost by participating in him, not by understanding him as a proposition. While theology involves both "action" and "contemplation," the Scriptures do not foster division between the two. A life of sacrifice enables contemplation of Christ's Passion - and contemplation of Christ's Passion empowers a life of sacrifice. This unity of the theological discipline is recovered in a participatory, sacramental ontology.

Biblical Interpretation ought not solely be based on the scientific method. While the historical-critical method (which builds on the scientific method) is one starting point for interpretation, it is merely the beginning of understanding the Bible in light of its allegorical, moral, and analogical interpretations which also illuminate Christ's redemptive work. Furthermore, the "Bible's home is the Church, not the academy" (138). The purpose of the scriptures, like the purpose of theology, is initiation into the life of the Trinity and not mere intellectual abstraction.

Philosophical Truth should not primarily be concerned with the rational comprehension of propositional statements. The knowledge of Truth is experienced by participating in the divine mystery of Christ, which far surpasses human comprehension. Boersma expresses this point by summarizing Gregory of Nyssa in stating: "No matter how much we progress in virtue and thus in the knowledge of God, God always remains greater" (162). While humans can know things about God through virtue and reason, this knowledge about God is only possible by analogy since God supersedes all human categories.

Tradition (i.e. the creeds and councils of the Church) maintains a participatory understanding of time. History is neither linear nor cyclical, but finds its grounding and identity in Christ who unites all time (linear and cyclical) in himself. For when Christ assumed the temporal, his redemptive work on earth assumed the eternal. As Boersma puts it, "In [Christ], the eternal Word enters into the temporal succession of events, thus allowing time to participate sacramentally in eternity" (127). If all of time participates in Christ's death, resurrection and ascension, then tradition flows from the same source as scripture because it is merely the outworking of Christ's redemption throughout history. Since this redemptive work sanctifies (and thus participates) in past, present, and future, we ought to regard tradition with reverence and deference since it comes "from the same divine wellspring" and points "towards the same goal" (Dei Verbum citation, 121).

The Church finds her unity in the Eucharist. By participating in Holy Communion, the three-fold body of Christ (the historical body, the Church as the body, and the bread and wine as the body) unites all things (earth, humanity, and the Kingdom of God) in Him who is the head of all creation (Ephesians 1.10). To recover the participatory nature of the Eucharist is to recover the unity of the Church. When the doctrine of the Eucharist is strengthened, the doctrine of the Church flowers because her identity as Corpus Christi takes on flesh and blood, thereby enabling her to be Christ's real presence in the world.

Hans Boersma pushes the boundaries of contemporary, Protestant scholarship by placing the treasures of evangelical spirituality within the context of a rich, sacramental worldview. Moreover, Boersma develops a fascinating understanding of how the Christian faith finds its source, fulfillment, and regeneration through sacramental participation in the redemptive work of Christ. Although his work offers an accurate diagnosis of the secularism which divides the Church, he posits few strategies for putting his corrective theology into practice. As an intrigued, evangelical reader, where am I supposed to find the "medicine of immortality" that Boersma prescribes for my sick soul? Is his blossoming romance with sacramental ontology an example of another evangelical on his way to a "Rome Sweet Home" conversion story or does his theology actually provide a seedbed for application within our evangelical churches?

In this reviewer's assessment, Boersma's treatment of the Reformation can towards being overly simplistic. For example, he argues that the Reformers made positive contributions towards "expositional preaching, Bible study, hymnody, and evangelical missions," yet ultimately failed in their project of reform because they "rent the supposedly seamless body of Christ in two" (87). But Boersma does consider providential role played in this historical "rending" of the body of Christ. After all, in the Old Testament, the Lord rent Israel into two kingdoms and later disciplined his covenant people by sending them into exile. It is questionable whether ought to be so quick to label the Reformation a failure when God has used similar events throughout salvation history to chastise and, indeed, introduce "reform" to his people. Thankfully for us, God has a track record for breathing life into dry bones.

Hans Boersma's book, starts a timely conversation about reform within evangelical Christianity. More specifically, this book is particularly valuable for those seeking an introduction to either patristic theology or to the twentieth century's Nouvelle Théologie movement. Furthermore, Boersma provides a concise history of theological ideas that is ideal for seminary students seeking a broad overview of how historical events and trends in philosophy have impacted the Church's doctrine. Because *Heavenly Participation* was written for a popular audience, academics seeking deep engagement with original sources are better served by Boersma's larger book, *Nouvelle Théologie & Sacramental Ontology: A Return to Mystery*, which was the fruit of his 2007-2008 sabbatical. Hans Boersma's theses have been nailed to the doors of Regent College; this reviewer suggests that evangelicals ought to be good "Bereans," examining the scriptures to see if what he says is true (Acts 17.11).

John Burtka
Trinity Forum Academy

***God, Sexuality, and the Self: An Essay 'On the Trinity.'* By Sarah Coakley. New York: Cambridge University Press, 2013, 365pp.**

Sarah Coakley, Anglican priest and Norris-Hulse Professor of Divinity at the University of Cambridge, has brought together various avenues of her scholarship into the first installment of a planned four-volume systematic theology (entitled *On Desiring God*). Future volumes will attend to the themes of theological anthropology and race (vol. 2), sin and atonement in conversation with hospitals and prisons (vol. 3), and Christology via the eucharist (vol. 4). The present volume draws from and extends the work in her *Powers and Submissions: Spirituality, Philosophy, and Gender* (2002), as well as edited volumes *Re-thinking Gregory of Nyssa* (2003) and *Re-thinking Dionysius the Areopagite* (2009). She describes the book's method using a term she coins: *théologie totale*, an interdisciplinary approach that resides "at the intersection of the theological, the political, the spiritual, and the sexual" (xvi-xvii). Thus, her overarching aim is to link often fragmented goals and discourses: the theoretical and the pastoral, the spiritual and the intellectual.

The main thrust of this volume is that a proper understanding of the Trinity requires deep attention to concerns about gender and desire. Indeed, for Coakley, human love and desire are grounded in the divine eros that characterizes the Triune God. With regard to human yearning, this trinitarian vision of desire has an ordering as well as a purgative function, both directing humanity toward the true object of its desire and countering all forms of idolatry that might obstruct this movement. For centuries, Coakley argues, issues of sexuality and desire have been seen as ancillary to any robust theological project. However, she boldly declares that our theological understanding of God is deficient if desire is left behind from the start. What Coakley calls the "modern textbook tradition" almost exclusively sees the pressing question for the first four centuries of Christianity to be the Son's relationship with the Father (e.g., focusing on issues of Arianism, Nestorianism, Eutychianism, as well as the nature of Chalcedonian orthodoxy). In contrast, she contends that attention to the often messy theological developments regarding the Spirit can reveal "the crucial prayer-based logic of emergent trinitarianism" (4).

Coakley's argument is deployed in seven distinct, yet deeply related chapters. The first two offer methodological reflections on the nature of systematic theology and the need for feminism and social sciences in that work. Chapter one responds to the contemporary aversion (often through philosophical, political, and feminist avenues) to systematic theology. Coakley responds to each critique, arguing ultimately that systematics (a modern conception of the theological task) should be properly apophatic, attentive to the marginalized 'other,' and fully embodied. Moreover, systematic theology must sharpen its focus on desire, understanding important theological themes (e.g., creation, fall, redemption, and eschatology) and devotional practices (e.g., contemplative prayer) to be unavoidably intertwined with gender and sexuality. Thus, the Spirit works to transgress the inherent binaries of Father/Son or Creator/creation. Here, the Spirit's interruptive or purgative work is seen when twoness "is divinely ambushed by threeness" (58). Gender, then, becomes a vehicle for participation in the life of God, displaying its openness to transfiguration.

Chapter two invokes a pair of watery metaphors to describe the work of contemporary theology. Rather than the receding sea of faith found on the shores of Matthew Arnold's *Dover Beach*, Coakley suggests that the deceptively illusory satisfaction of three prevalent Wigan Piers ("high, authoritarian ecclesiastical Christian 'orthodoxy'", a new postmodern theological metanarrative, and liberal feminist theology) beckons theologians. Each attempts to engage theology with social science but fails to recover "a creative *and* critical relation of theology to the social sciences" (76). *Théologie totale*, with its attention on the 'other' and embrace of ascetic contemplation, should open up space for the crucial social and political questions of gender and power without reducing theology to either. In concluding the chapter with nine characteristics of this theological approach, Coakley underscores the rich apophatic dimension of her theological project.

Chapter three treats the development of Trinitarian dogma by noting the inherent fluidity in early Christian understanding of the members of the Godhead. Thus, limiting one's focus to conciliar statements could bring the Holy Spirit into sharp contrast with and/or subordination to the Father and the Son. Coakley's alternative centers on a prayer-based model of the Trinity grounded in Paul's words in Romans 8, where the Spirit receives both logical and experiential priority. This model, which Coakley observes in the apostolic period, prevents Trinitarian orthodoxy from being reduced to simplistic formulas. Through examining the work of Origen and Athanasius, she shows that reflections on prayer result in implications for understanding the Spirit, and that questions of the Spirit's movement lead to questions about gender roles and societal order.

Chapter four offers insights into how sociological fieldwork might be integrated into systematic theology through Coakley's observations of two ecclesial groups (an Anglican charismatic parish and a sectarian charismatic community) with regard to their engagement with and understanding of the Spirit. Chapter five brings art to the conversation by including thirty-nine artistic images of the Trinity (ranging from classical icons to seemingly nonconformist depictions), with each presenting the members and the relations of the Godhead in a variety of ways. Coakley describes this as a "visual and imaginative 'magical mystery tour'" (192). This engagement with the creative aspects of doctrine allows for a playful freedom that can challenge static theological notions and reified constructions while also generating new and theologically fertile icons of the Triune God. By presenting these works as theology (therefore, with limited commentary), Coakley underscores the Christian tradition's comfort both with an image-based apophaticism and a welcoming of creative and unorthodox artistic ideas.

In chapter six, which attempts to reinvigorate the Trinitarian theology of Gregory of Nyssa and Augustine of Hippo, Coakley aims to show that the major voices of the Christian tradition have embraced what she calls "the 'messy entanglement' of sexual desire and desire for God" (272-273), with the theological vision of each emerging in an ecstatic moment that exceeds their categories for both Trinitarian relations and gender. This new sense of Augustinian eros leads her to reevaluate John Donne's sonnet "Batter My Heart, Three-Person'd God." Chapter seven discusses apophasis and desire. The work of Pseudo-

Dionysius (which has resided beneath the surface of much of the argument) is here explicitly treated. The Areopagite deploys seemingly contradictory visual metaphors of circular motion and hierarchical ordering to image the Creator/creation relationship. Following this patristic guide, Coakley argues that the centrality of divine eros (as both ontology and itinerary) grounds a purgative moment regarding gendered language for God. The book concludes with six summary theses that recall the interconnection between God, desire, and prayer that animates the book as a whole and issues a final encouragement to pursue the Triune God in contemplative prayer.

Readers and lovers of systematic theology will appreciate Coakley's work in redeeming a discipline that had been abandoned by many. However, this is not static theological work since *"théologie totale* continually risks destabilization and redirection" (48). Indeed, her claim is that systematics is fundamentally contemplative, offering "practices of un-mastery" that lead us on the way to participation in the divine life. Moreover, this book excels in bringing desire to the forefront of theological discourse. In American theology in particular, questions of desire have been left to discussions of ethics, often by relying on a dualistic conception of terms such as eros and agape (whether mediated through CS Lewis or Anders Nygren). Like Benedict XVI (in *Deus Caritas Est*), Coakley masterfully highlights the centrality of divine desire in Trinitarian doctrine, setting eros at the heart of the Christian life.

Coakley acknowledges at various points that her *théologie totale* involves significant risk, in part because its interdisciplinary approach renders it vulnerable to criticism from more than one arena. Settled experts in gender studies or ethnography or aesthetics could no doubt highlight various lacunae in the discussions. For instance, readers looking for a detailed treatment of various expressions of human sexual identity or the more troubled intersections of religion and sexuality (e.g., clergy sexual abuse) will be disappointed. But, on balance, addressing such broader issues is not Coakley's aim, and the theological roadwork here undertaken could readily facilitate deeper engagements along these lines.

Overall, the method and substance of Coakley's theology are both challenging and rewarding. The book also includes several significant pedagogical features, such as the thorough bibliographic sections at the end of each chapter (offering further reading regarding theology, gender studies, social science, and aesthetics, as well as source information regarding Coakley's in-chapter conversation partners). She also has included a glossary of key terms, heightening the sense that she wanted to make the volume engaging for non-specialists—a goal that, while commendable, is necessarily frustrated by the complex nature of Coakley's theological undertaking. Nonetheless, this volume is of great service to theologians and graduate students as well as those involved in the wider disciplines Coakley engages.

Derek C. Hatch
Howard Payne University

Augustine's Theology of Preaching by Peter T. Sanlon. Fortress Press, 2014. 200pp.

In *Augustine's Theology of Preaching*, Peter T. Sanlon seeks to redress the imbalance in Augustinian scholarship wherein most research focuses on the Bishop of Hippo Regius' more philosophical theology or commentaries on Scripture, rarely if ever applying theological scrutiny to his large corpus of sermons. Sanlon laments that, instead of looking at

Augustine as the active preacher and pastor he was, scholars continually turn to the same few works systematic or thematic theology time and again. However, Augustine was a regular preacher, a dynamic and engaging orator who was also active pastorally. Therefore, if we are to hope to fully grasp the complete range and significance of this giant of western theology, we must grasp his theology of preaching. This Sanlon sets out to do, lending balance to the scholarly scales and beginning to fill an important gap in acadmeic approaches to Augustine.

After an Introduction discussing the goals of the project, Chapter One sets Augustine in his historical setting of late fourth- and early fifth-century Africa. However, much of the nuance of Late Roman historiography and of the ongoing tensions between change and consistency that characterise this period is absent from Sanlon's treatment. The chapter is not able to convincingly situate Roman North Africa in Late Antiquity, since Africa's entire history feels like it has been collapsed into a single moment, as if it all is of equal relevance to Augustine's Late Imperial context. This sort of historical generalisation and characterisation could be balanced by references to key work historical works on Africa in this period (e.g. Guy Halsall, *Barbarian Migrations and the Roman West* [2007], or Chris Wickham, *Framing the Early Middle Ages* [2005]). While Sanlon's wider observations that North Africa exhibited many contrasting impulses between chaos and order, Roman and non-Roman, are true, what such observations lack is the degree of nuance found in the literature of Classicist and Mediaevalist alike in the field of Late Antiquity.

This chapter also includes brief but helpful introductions to Ambrose, Tertullian, Cyprian, and Peter Chrysologus, commenting on how the first three may have influenced Augustine, and contrasting Chrysologus' preaching style to Augustine's in the next generation. These brief details on other western preachers are useful in situating Augustine in his context. However, Chrysologus could have been given a bit more analysis and Sanlon questionable states that by Chrysologus' day, 'the Roman Empire no longer held preeminence' (11). Chrysologus died in 450, and the Roman Empire, while certainly diminished from its foregoing splendour, certainly still held *preeminence* at the time, given that even the barbarian kings that had established themselves as distinct entities in former Roman territories such as Africa derived much of their power from engagement with the political, social, and economic structures of the Western Roman Empire (not to mention the still strong Eastern Roman Empire). In Chrysologus' day, this preeminence would have been especially visible in a city such as Ravenna, where the imperial court was resident throughout much of Chrysologus' tenure as bishop.

After situating Augustine in his historical context, Sanlon sets out to situate him in his *oratorical* context. Sanlon discusses the impact of Gorgias, Plato, Cicero, Quintilian, and Apuleius on Augustine; his analysis effectively demonstrates how these figures helped shape Augustine's thought by the time he was preaching in the 390s. Most importantly, Augustine had realised that simple persuasion was insufficient, and that, beyond any knowledge or personal good conduct, one needed an ultimate authority to help bring people to an acknowledgement and appreciation of the truth, to be persuaded to live by it. Despite all of his "pagan" training, the only place Augustine found the necessary authority to make oratory truly effective in persuading people and helping them find truth and live by it was in the Christian scriptures, and with these he engaged constantly in his career as a preacher.

In Chapter Three, Sanlon discusses Augustine's *De Doctrina Christiana* as an important piece of background for the sermons. One of the key points that emerges from this discussion is that Augustine wrote *De Doctrina* as a training manual for preachers but that he felt that his training in pagan oratory was not sufficient for such a task. Therefore, Augustine left Book Four of the work unfinished for thirty years before writing it, having only then gained the experience he thought necessary to train preachers – decades of preaching and immersion in the Bible. As noted, scripture became for Augustine the ultimate authority for effective, transformative rhetoric.

In Chapter Four, we learn about interiority and temporality, these being the hermeneutical lenses which Sanlon had promised in the Introduction to use in his analysis of Augustine. Interiority is approached through four strands of Augustine's thought: self-reflection, the inner teacher, the heart, and hierarchical ordering. Sanlon cogently argues that the revolution in Augustine's thought concerning the heart in the 390s was not the result of the *Confessions*, but, rather, of Augustine launching his career as a preacher and immersing himself in the Psalter, on which he preached extensively through the decade. Sanlon ends up defining interiority as 'the inner realm of desirous longing, evaluation and prayer' (81). Temporality is approached through the motifs of created matter, time itself, and journeying, bringing us to the definition of temporality as 'the successive flow and teleological development of God's plan for creation from beginning to consummation' (86). Having defined these two key hermeneutical principles, Sanlon engages with Coleen Hoffman Gowans, Paul Ricoeur, and Charles Taylor, and their readings of temporality and Augustine's *Sermons* before moving into his final chapters of analysis.

These final chapters are the best in the book. Sanlon moves from discussing overarching concerns and turns to actually analysing the *Sermons*. In Chapters Five through Seven, he conducts an inductive analysis of the *Sermons* concerning the issues of riches and money, death and resurrection, and relationships. Here we see interiority and temporality applied to scripture and addressed to the congregation of Hippo. Here we see a variety of Augustine's other theological insights applied to a living body of Christian people; we also see all of Sanlon's earlier discussions – order and chaos, oratory and Scripture, interiority and temporality – finally free at play in the midst of Augustine's work itself. One is tempted to wish there were more of it, but, then,erhaps we should, if stirred by these analyses, go out and read the *Sermones ad Populum* for ourselves, bringing with us the equipment provided by Sanlon.

In conclusion, *Augustine's Theology of Preaching* is an interesting and well-developed discussion that should help newcomers to the *Sermones ad Populum* enter more fully into the theological underpinnings of St. Augustine's preaching and help those already familiar with the content return to it with fresh insights and new eyes. This is one of the most important jobs performed by any scholar of any ancient literature, enabling readers to engage more fully with the ancient texts themselves. Whatever reservations this reviewer may have about some of the representations of the Later Roman Empire, Sanlon achieves this higher goal. He does so by implementing the two hermeneutical keys of interiority and temporality, formulating a discussion that brings along and touches upon other famous Augustinian concerns in the sermons, such as order, love, the heart, and friendship. Sanlon also provides the pastoral application from these sermons of Augustine's teachings on topics such as slavery, women, and predestination. Thus, not only is the reader invited to explore

Augustine's theology *of* preaching, he or she is also drawn into an exploration of Augustine's theology *through* preaching.

Matthew Hoskin
University of Edinburgh

Evangelical Faith and the Challenge of Historical Criticism. **Edited by Christopher M. Hays and Christopher B. Ansberry. Grand Rapids, Mich.: Baker Academic, 2013. 241 pp.**

What would happen to evangelical faith if historical-critical dogma became orthodox for Christianity? Hays and Ansberry assembled a crew of scholars to address this important question. While it is no secret that evangelical and critical scholars operate with two different worldviews (at least in their interpretation of the Bible), evangelicals are constantly faced with the question of whether this or that result is true or helpful, even though it was derived from historical-critical investigation. This tension is perhaps felt more acutely in Old Testament studies, where dating conclusions are in constant flux and authorship is dogmatically refused to the authors ascribed by tradition. This edited volume proceeds by hypothetically accepts various historical-critical dogmas and then explores whether Evangelical faith remains intact. I should note that this hypothetical nature of the book creates some ambiguity regarding the authors' actual beliefs, which are not always made explicit.

Hays and Herring begin with a hypothetically ahistorical Adam and inquire whether original sin (both the imputation of sinful nature and guilt) holds true. They argue that original guilt is not the correct reading of Romans 5 and suggest that the concupiscence in Jam 1:13-15 is a better hamartiology. James 1, in conjunction with their reading of Romans 5, eliminates the need for an originating sin of a historical Adam and for original guilt. They make a rather unconvincing attempt to explain the source of sin by sociological phenomena, while ignoring the question of how it actually originated, which is a major lacuna in the chapter.

Ansberry presents minimalist and maximalist views of the historicity of the Exodus narrative, then explores the implications of the minimalist view for evangelicals. He suggests that the narrative is concerned with the meaning of the event, not with portraying the reality of how it happened (66). The Exodus was a historical event that grew mythologically through cultural memory (66-67). The cultural memory matters more for Israel than how it actually happened. He argues that their historical occurrence is "essential" (70), but that we must only maintain that God delivered Israel from Egypt in some way, whether it corresponds to the biblical account or not.

Ansberry and Hwang explore the consequences of supposing Deuteronomy and covenant theology arose in exile. They suggest the "content of the material" is the locus of authority, not the author, and that it is "clear" Deuteronomy was compiled in the post-Mosaic era, though citing only Deut 1:1-5 as evidence (84-85). With a text-centered hermeneutic and an appeal to the Holy Spirit (86), they conclude Deuteronomy contains the "Mosaic *traditum*" (86).

Warhurst, Tarrer, and Hays explore those thorny Old Testament prophecies that seem to lie unfulfilled. They explain discrepancies in prophecies via assumptions of redactive practice (i.e. a later author added corrections to the original prophecy when it seemed to fail, e.g., Ezek 29:18-19), and they further suppose later generations appropriated unfulfilled prophecies typologically (e.g., Isa 7:14). Prophecy's goal is not foretelling, but expressing God's ultimate governance over creation (100). Prophecy is not concerned much with a timetable, and fulfillment is conditional (102-03). *Vaticinium ex eventu* prophecy is typical of the ancient Near East and therefore is no threat to find in Daniel. What vindicates prophecy is not its true historical fulfillment, but its inclusion in the canon, because the Holy Spirit "inspired, preserved, and presented [them] to us" (112). The authors explain unfulfilled prophecies as deferral of prophetic fulfillment due to the behavior of Israel or their enemies (113-22). This suggestion has promise, although it need not apply in every case.

Ansberry, Strine, Klink, and Lincicum explore pseudepigraphy with further appeals to the Holy Spirit as the guarantee that our Bible is inspired, no matter who wrote the documents (130-31). They raise the issue of stated authorship (John 12:41, citing Isa 6:10 and 53:10), but then dismiss it by claiming "ancient conceptions of authorship and those of our modern context" exhibit "substantial variation" (140). They suggest we should not subject Scripture to "our own autonomous standard of perfection," but should seek "the perfection Scripture has in a historically a posteriori act of discipleship" (155). Of course, to claim that evangelicals force standards of perfection on a document (e.g., Paul must have written all 13 letters) is to beg the question.

The last two chapters, which cover the historical Jesus and the Paul of Acts and his letters, are surprisingly conservative. Daling and Hays hold that, even if some miracles are theological constructions, Jesus' historical performance of miracles is essential for our faith (169). They implicate Dunn's adoptionist Christology as "at the very [least] a heretical construal of the deity of Christ" (173). They "eschew" those who deny the virgin birth (174). Similarly, the historical resurrection is essential to our faith and they reject the possibility of an "objective vision" (that God caused visions of Jesus in the minds of the apostles). Although each author is different, one gets the impression that evangelicals are less tolerable to historical-critics who mess with Jesus. Lastly, Kuecker and Liebengood, on the Paul of Acts and his letters, suggest the Acts 15 and Galatians 1-2 issue is "not impossible to resolve with a certain degree of satisfaction if one feels the need to do so" (186). They suggest those who find two different Pauls in Acts and his letters have not considered enough "issues of audience, genre and occasion" (198).

Evangelicals should appreciate the authors for producing this work. It provides a live illustration of the consequences of succumbing to historical-critical dogma. And while each reader will evaluate this attempt differently, I found this to be a failed project, for reasons which I will categorize and explain. First is the constant attempt to place inspired meaning in the writing, rather than the author. If we suppose that Deuteronomy was created in the seventh century BC with a political agenda by an author who was not a prophet, using Moses' voice, then the original meaning of the document involves a political power play. To suppose Deuteronomy later becomes inspired when it is included in the canon is to suppose that the fictitious world created by the original authors becomes the "real world" for readers of the canonical Deuteronomy. In other words, the document changes meaning based upon its canon. Such a theory is reminiscent of the New Criticism literary theory, which has been criticized heavily by literary critics, notoriously by E. D. Hirsch, Jr. in *Validity in Interpretation* (New Haven, CT: Yale University Press, 1967), and even by historical-critical biblical scholar John Barton in *Reading the Old Testament: Method in Biblical Study* (Rev. ed.; Louisville, Ky.: Westminster John Knox, 1996). While this is not the place to argue that meaning cannot be tied only to a text, the point here is that the authors of this work failed to discuss this fundamental hermeneutical issue. Aside from the philosophical issue, the Bible was concerned with authorship (e.g., Lev 26:46; 2 Thess 2:1-2; 3:17), as was the early church who set apostolicity as a standard of canonicity.

A second, but related issue is their constant punting to the Holy Spirit to save pseudepigraphal documents as Christian revelation (86; 130-31). They suggest that canonicity implies the document's inspiration by the Holy Spirit and that he guided it to the canon. However, this is a strange anti-rationalistic turn in a thoroughgoing rationalistic project. Scripture claims to be inspired, but the classic statement (2 Tim 3:16) is in a disputed Pauline letter. Thus, even the clear self-attestations of Scripture to inspiration may only be power plays (like Deuteronomy), an attempt to legitimate one's own pseudepigraphal letter with a claim to inspiration. So how can the authors believe that the Holy Spirit inspired these writings (and did he inspire the original meaning, or the canonical meaning)? What evidence suggests such a phenomenon? Moreover, to believe a document is only inspired because it landed in the canon is to place authority in the final redactor rather than in the text, since the text would lack authority apart from the redactor's decision to include the writing. On the other hand, we could believe Scripture's self-attestations to inspiration are trustworthy, but more importantly for this issue, that the biblical authors were mostly, if not all, prophets. Moses, Samuel, the major and minor prophets, David, the apostles, and perhaps other biblical authors (Solomon? Hebrews? Luke?) were endowed with the Holy Spirit as prophets of God, hence we know that God channeled revelation through them. Such a position could be considered a more rational reason to believe Scripture contains prophetic revelation from God, and in that respect could be more "critical" than some of the authors of this work.

A third issue relates to exegesis and argumentation, which sometimes leave something to be desired. For example, on p. 61 Ansberry suggests Ramesses II cannot be the pharaoh of the Exodus because he "lies entombed, not at the bottom of the Sea of Reeds but in the National Museum in Cairo." But Exodus nowhere says pharaoh drowned in the sea, only his troops. Page 62 claims "not even the Bible paints a univocal picture of the exodus event," but only Pss 78 and 105 are cited, which are may be explained as poetic developments and interpretations of the historical narrative in Exodus. The discussion of unfulfilled prophecies completely ignores premodern and evangelical solutions. For example, the change from Tyre to Egypt in the prophecy of destruction (Ezek 29:18-19) could possibly be explained by a theological assumption of Ezekiel, such as corporate solidarity, or a number of other possibilities. But the authors simply assume v. 19 is a redactional addendum after the prophecy in v. 18 failed. I noted earlier the skirting of the issue of stated authorship by a simple claim to a difference in views of authorship from the premodern to the modern era (140), but this ignores premodern Jewish and Christian obsession with ascribing biblical books to singular, prophetic authors. These are only a few examples of the tendency to ignore contrary evidence, to mistake what the biblical text actually says, to make sweeping generalizations without proper support, and to ignore competing interpretations. These sorts of problems seem common in the attempt to harmonize the conclusions of historical-criticism with Evangelical faith.

At the root of these problems is, I conjecture, the definition of historical-criticism as a "tool" (19, 205) by Hays and Ansberry (although Hays may be responsible for the definition, since he was the sole author of p. 19). Historical-criticism uses many tools—redaction criticism, source criticism, literary methods, sociological analysis, comparative study—but historical-criticism is not a tool. It is an approach to interpretation that necessarily entails a worldview. This anti-supernatural worldview was defined classically by E. Troeltsch, who expounded the principles of doubt, analogy, and correlation, which effectively ruled out any explanations of Scripture that involved supernaturalism. Therefore, historical-criticism is not a tool, wielded by Baur, Troeltsch, and Bultmann and then handed off to the evangelical to try his hand at more academically respectable results. But have evangelicals benefitted from historical-critical investigation? That is another question, but a brief answer must admit that historical-critics have caused all biblical scholars to investigate further the historical and human dimension of Scripture. But one might argue that biblical historical investigation achieves best results under evangelical assumptions, rather than critical assumptions, such that the former may thank the latter for driving focus to the historical, but evangelicals need not absorb critical conclusions or methods. Lastly, these comments are not intended to indict the authors, whose positions are sometimes hypothetical and sometimes unclear, but rather to dialogue with the authors in the same irenic spirit in which they wrote the book. I recommend all students and scholars wrestling with this issue read this work in order to evaluate for themselves the effort to harmonize the two approaches to Scripture.

Todd A. Scacewater
Westminster Theological Seminary

ECUMENICAL CREEDS OF THE CHRISTIAN FAITH

The Apostles' Creed (Old Roman Form)

I believe in God the Father Almighty. And in Jesus Christ his only Son our Lord, who was born of the Holy Spirit and the Virgin Mary; crucified under Pontius Pilate and buried; the third day he rose from the dead; he ascended into heaven, and sits at the right hand of the Father, from thence he shall come to judge the quick and the dead. And in the Holy Spirit; the holy Church; the forgiveness of sins; [and] the resurrection of the flesh.

The Nicæno-Constantinopolitan Creed

I believe in one God, the Father Almighty, Maker of heaven and earth, and of all things visible and invisible.

And in one Lord Jesus Christ, the only-begotten Son of God, begotten of His Father before all worlds, God of God, Light of Light, very God of very God, begotten, not made, being of one substance with the Father; by whom all things were made; who for us men, and for our salvation, came down from heaven, and was incarnate by the Holy Ghost of the Virgin Mary, and was made man, and was crucified also for us under Pontius Pilate; He suffered and was buried; and the third day He rose again, according to the Scriptures; and ascended into heaven, and sitteth on the right hand of the Father; and He shall come again with glory to judge both the quick and the dead; whose kingdom shall have no end.

And I believe in the Holy Ghost, the Lord and Giver of life, who proceedeth from the Father and the Son; who with the Father and the Son together is worshipped and glorified; who spake by the Prophets. And I believe in one holy Christian and apostolic Church. I acknowledge one Baptism for the remission of sins; and I look for the resurrection of the dead, and the life of the world to come. Amen.

The Athanasian Creed

Whoever desires to be saved must above all things hold to the catholic faith. Unless a man keeps it in its entirety inviolate, he will assuredly perish eternally.

Now this is the catholic faith, that we worship one God in trinity and trinity in unity, without either confusing the persons, or dividing the substance. For the Father's person is one, the Son's another, the Holy Spirit's another; but the Godhead of the Father, the Son, and the Holy Spirit is one, their glory is equal, their majesty is co-eternal.

Such as the Father is, such is the Son, such is also the Holy Spirit. The Father is uncreate, the Son uncreate, the Holy Spirit uncreate. The Father is infinite, the Son infinite, the Holy Spirit infinite. The Father is eternal, the Son eternal, the Holy Spirit eternal. Yet there are not three eternals, but one eternal; just as there are not three uncreates or three infinites, but one uncreate and one infinite. In the same way the Father is almighty, the Son almighty, the Holy Spirit almighty; yet there are not three almighties, but one almighty.

Thus the Father is God, the Son God, the Holy Spirit God; and yet there are not three Gods, but there is one God. Thus the Father is Lord, the Son Lord, the Holy Spirit Lord; and yet there are not three Lords, but there is one Lord. Because just as we are compelled by

Christian truth to acknowledge each person separately to be both God and Lord, so we are forbidden by the catholic religion to speak of three Gods or Lords.

The Father is from none, not made nor created nor begotten. The Son is from the Father alone, not made nor created but begotten. The Holy Spirit is from the Father and the Son, not made nor created nor begotten but proceeding. So there is one Father, not three Fathers; one Son, not three Sons; one Holy Spirit, not three Holy Spirits. And in this trinity there is nothing before or after, nothing greater or less, but all three persons are co-eternal with each other and co-equal. Thus in all things, as has been stated above, both trinity and unity and unity in trinity must be worshipped. So he who desires to be saved should think thus of the Trinity.

It is necessary, however, to eternal salvation that he should also believe in the incarnation of our Lord Jesus Christ. Now the right faith is that we should believe and confess that our Lord Jesus Christ, the Son of God, is equally both God and man.

He is God from the Father's substance, begotten before time; and He is man from His mother's substance, born in time. Perfect God, perfect man composed of a human soul and human flesh, equal to the Father in respect of His divinity, less than the Father in respect of His humanity.

Who, although He is God and man, is nevertheless not two, but one Christ. He is one, however, not by the transformation of His divinity into flesh, but by the taking up of His humanity into God; one certainly not by confusion of substance, but by oneness of person. For just as soul and flesh are one man, so God and man are one Christ.

Who suffered for our salvation, descended to hell, rose from the dead, ascended to heaven, sat down at the Father's right hand, from where He will come to judge the living and the dead; at whose coming all men will rise again with their bodies, and will render an account of their deeds; and those who have done good will go to eternal life, those who have done evil to eternal fire.

This is the catholic faith. Unless a man believes it faithfully and steadfastly, he cannot be saved. Amen

The Definition of Chalcedon

We, then, following the holy Fathers, all with one consent, teach men to confess one and the same Son, our Lord Jesus Christ, the same perfect in Godhead and also perfect in manhood; truly God and truly man, of a reasonable soul and body; consubstantial with the Father according to the Godhead, and consubstantial with us according to the Manhood; in all things like unto us, without sin; begotten before all ages of the Father according to the Godhead, and in these latter days, for us and for our salvation, born of the Virgin Mary, the Mother of God, according to the Manhood; one and the same Christ, Son, Lord, Only-begotten, to be acknowledged in two natures, inconfusedly, unchangeably, indivisibly, inseparably; the distinction of natures being by no means taken away by the union, but rather the property of each nature being preserved, and concurring in one Person and one Subsistence, not parted or divided into two persons, but one and the same Son, and only begotten, God the Word, the Lord Jesus Christ, as the prophets from the beginning have declared concerning him, and the Lord Jesus Christ himself has taught us, and the Creed of the holy Fathers has handed down to us.

www.ingramcontent.com/pod-product-compliance
Lightning Source LLC
Chambersburg PA
CBHW051708090426
42736CB00013B/2602